T

A HANDFUL OF DUST

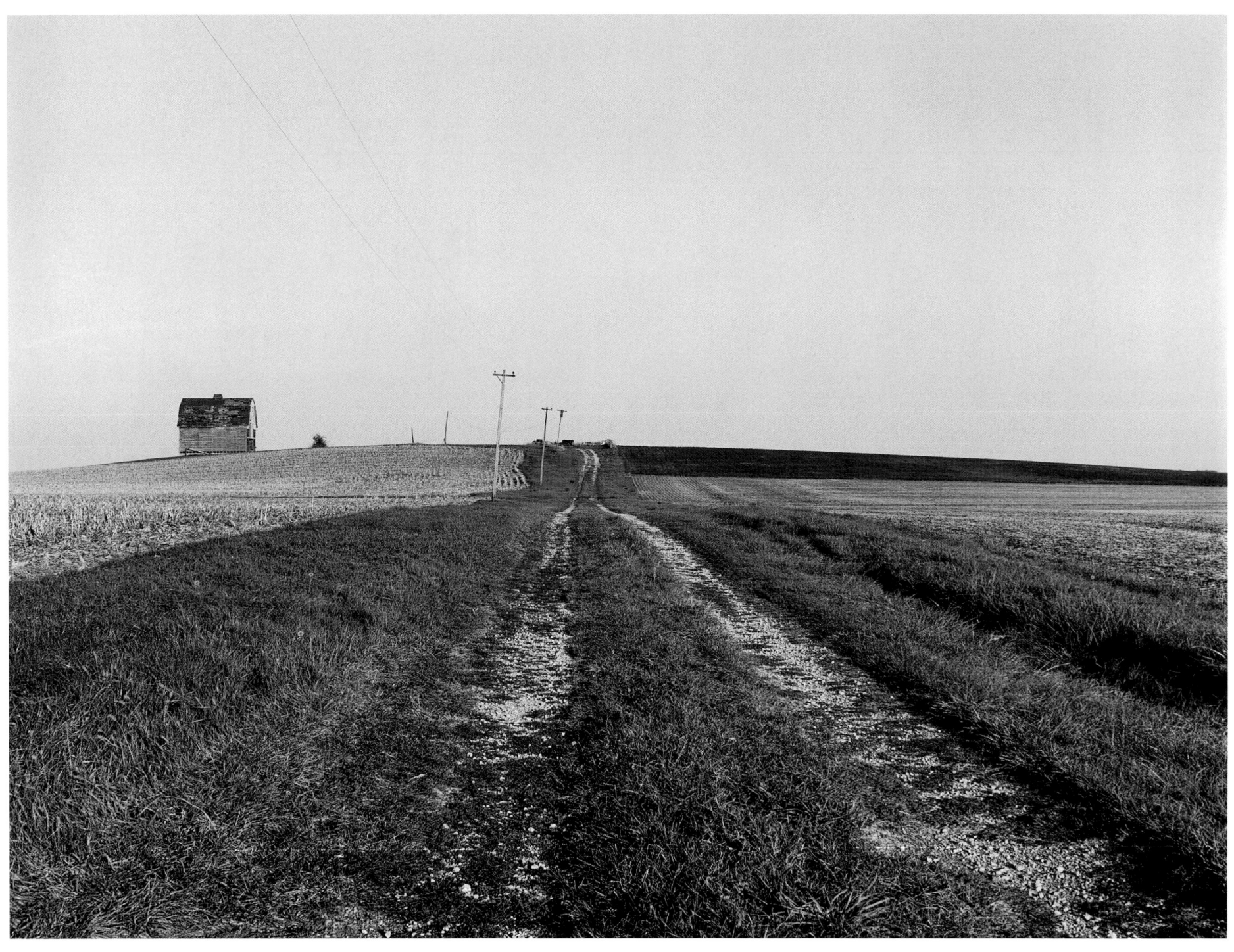

DAVID PLOWDEN

A Handful of Dust

Photographs
of Disappearing
America

W.W. Norton & Company

New York • London

A Handful of Dust: Photographs of Disappearing America
David Plowden

Copyright © 2006 by David Plowden
All rights reserved
Printed in The United Kingdom
First Edition

Page 21: Epigraph from "The Waste Land," *T.S. Eliot Collected Poems, 1909–1962,*
Harcourt, Brace & World, Inc., New York, 1963.

The text of this book is composed in FF Thesis, The Mix (FontFont)
With the display in Antique Condensed–Two (The Font Bureau)
Book design and composition by John Bernstein Design, Inc., New York
Manufacturing by Balding & Mansell, Norwich, England

Library of Congess Cataloging-in-Publication Data

Plowden, David.
A handful of dust photographs of disappearing America / David Plowden.

        p.   cm.
ISBN: 0-393-06033-0 (hardcover)

1. Photography, Artistic. 2. United States—Pictorial works. I. Title.

TR654.P57   2005
779'.9973—dc22   2005020777

W. W. Norton & Company, 500 Fifth Avenue, New York NY 10110
www.wwnorton.com

W. W. Norton & Company Ltd., Castle House, 75/76 Wells Street, London, W1T 3QT

1 2 3 4 5 6 7 8 9 0

FRONTISPIECE:
Detail from plate 46 [Owego Township, Livingston County, Illinois (2003)]

TABLE OF CONTENTS

FOR SANDRA

INTRODUCTION

The sea of corn and soybeans still rolled on, covering the land in every direction and farmsteads seen in the distance gave the impression that everything was the same. I once knew this part of Iowa like the palm of my hand. I had felt at home there. But not today. In the eighteen years since I had last been here, the transformation was almost unimaginable. When you slowed down, drove off on any given section road and looked closely you realized that altogether too many farms were abandoned. The land had been plowed up to the dooryards. All sorts of derelict rusted farm machinery was strewn haphazardly among the weeds. Screens in kitchen doors were in tatters. In the stillness one could imagine the voices of children playing. The barns were gone to rack and ruin; gaunt reminders of when there were cats drinking warm milk from a cracked dish in the corner and where, in the winter, the windows were always steamy from the warmth within. One could hear the sound of cows munching while they were being milked. The barns were ruins now, cold and lifeless with the wind blowing through the broken boards.

We stopped in Guernsey one evening in hopes of finding Marion Baustian's garage, where my students and I spent most of a day in 1986. What we found was a crumbling derelict, a carcass. Just enough remained intact for me to recognize it. It looked as if it had been closed for decades. Perhaps it had. Aside from Marion, the thing I remember best about his place was a sign hanging over the cash register which left no doubt about his feelings. I'D RATHER BE FISHING, it proclaimed in block capitals. I hoped he'd finally been granted his wish.

We walked up the stone steps to the door of the old Victorian Hotel Brooklyn on Front Street and rang the bell. There was a long wait, so I rang again and heard a voice saying, "I'm coming." The door opened and there was Kay Lawson with a cane in hand. We introduced ourselves and I told her that years ago I had spent the afternoon taking pictures of the upstairs bedrooms and the bathroom. At one point her young daughter had come looking for me—"She said you had wondered if I were all right." She smiled and said she remembered—whether she did or not didn't seem to matter. She was most cordial. I asked if we could look upstairs. She reached for the banister and started up the long staircase. It was then that we realized that she was almost totally blind. Nonetheless, she insisted on escorting us. "I know my way around," she said reassuringly. "We've been on the National Register of Historic Places since 1966," she added proudly. "But the insurance people told me to tear down the ivy off the walls, said it was a fire hazard, so I decided it was time to close."

At dusk Sandra and I drove into the town of Victor. I was very ambivalent about going there but it was on our way to the Holiday Inn. I knew that John and Violet Van Waus had closed their clothing store in 1987. I had also heard that Ted Bohstedt, the owner of the grain elevator and feed mill in town, had sold his establishment. I heard from someone that he was dead. I really didn't want to see Main Street or Van's; nonetheless, they were on the way through town and we couldn't avoid them. I tried not to look, but as we passed Van's I saw that the door and windows were boarded up with weathered plywood. Like so many other places of its kind I have known, it looked as if it had been closed forever.

I remember the first time I opened the door and introduced myself to the Van Wauses. I was transported way back in time to another world. Although you could buy Nerf Balls, Reeboks, and Hawkeye T-shirts in the front, as you got deeper into the store it became more and more of an anachronism. At the very back there was a shelf on which there was a box of buttons for high-button shoes. One of the features I remember best was an assortment of hats that must have represented at least half a century of styles. They were displayed in beautiful cases with accordion doors and beveled glass mirrors. I heard that the interior of the store went to a museum when the Van Wauses retired. There was also an unconfirmed rumor that a movie company bought the whole place lock, stock, and barrel and had it shipped to California.

Several years after the store closed, when John and Violet celebrated their fiftieth wedding anniversary, their children asked them what they might like as an anniversary gift. "To go to David Plowden's exhibition in Chicago," they answered. I could not believe it when I saw them at the opening or when they told me the story. Few times in my life I have ever been so touched. The next day I had to give a gallery talk and they came. I happened to be sitting on a stool in front the picture of the door to their store. Someone asked me a question about the photograph. I pointed to the back of the room and said that the owners of the store were in the audience and they could answer the question better than I.

Finding Victor was a lucky accident. While I was teaching at the University of Iowa, Steve McCombs, the best friend of my TA's husband, worked for Ted Bohstedt. One thing led to another, and to an introduction to Ted. The local feed store and feed mill, as well as the grain elevator, are a farming community's focal point. Bohstedt's was no exception. The front office to his mill was the gathering place for most of the local farmers. While Steve or one of the other men who worked for Ted loaded or unloaded trucks of feed and grain, the old-timers would play sheepshead by the hour in front of the window while they commented on any and all who passed by. I had never heard of sheepshead before and Ted and his cohorts did their best to teach me how to play. I never got the hang of it because the cards are ranked in such an arcane order. I subsequently learned that it is a Central European game akin to pinochle, euchre and skat invented by shepherds in the 1700s. The order of the cards reflects the fact that the peasants who developed it were perennially disgruntled with whoever was King, so they gave the kings in sheepshead a lower rank than queens and jacks.

Sheepshead was an important part of the daily routine at Bohstedt's, and because of all the hours I spent trying to master the rudiments of the game I became known to every farmer within a ten-mile radius of Victor. In the two years I spent there I was invited to photograph every farm in the vicinity.

It took a long time for Ted to accept me—he joked good-naturedly about "his resident photographer." At first I knew he considered me a nuisance but in time he accepted me and let me do what I wanted. By the spring of 1987 I had photographed everyone I knew in Victor except Ted. He was adamant: he did not want to have his picture taken. However, I was equally adamant about taking his portrait. I told Steve about the situation and we cooked up a ruse. Ted always had his lunch in the grain elevator office at precisely noon. So one day Steve and I walked into the office where Ted was quietly enjoying his sandwich. We locked the door behind us and told Ted we wouldn't let him out until I had taken his picture. He complained mightily all the while. Nonetheless, he posed for the better part of his lunch hour and I was able to make not one but two portraits of him.

In the winter of 1988 I had a show at the new Iowa State Museum in Des Moines to celebrate the publication of my book on Iowa, *A Sense of Place*. Virtually everyone I had been associated with during the four years I had been photographing Iowa came to my book signing. At one point someone put several books in front of me to sign. I heard a voice say, "You don't recognize me, do you?" I looked up and there was Ted dressed in a slightly ill-fitting suit. I had never seen him in anything but a pair of bib overalls.

The first time I was in Columbus Junction was in 1984, when I led a workshop for a group of twenty students from the University of Iowa. This workshop, which was supposed to last for ten days, went on for three months. I had drawn a map outlining the area of the town where one could photograph. Anything seen from there was fair game but the rule was your feet had to be within the boundaries. The one thing I told them was to leave their cameras behind for the first day or two. We know nothing about this place, I said, so walk around, tell anybody who asks you why you are here. Have a beer, lean over a fence, talk to them. If you jump out of the bus pointing your cameras at everyone and everything, you will be like a bunch of paid assassins. Everyone will flee.

Each day at one o'clock, after the noon crowd had cleared out, we would meet at the local restaurant to discuss what the students had seen, any problems, etc. Many of them were not from Iowa, but they found a way of gaining the town's trust—not an easy task. Two young women from Germany who had never been in America were driven directly from O'Hare to Columbus Junction to join us. In due course, Columbus Junction adopted us. The old hotel, which rented rooms only by the month, opened its doors to any of the students who didn't want to drive back and forth to Iowa City.

In 1984 Columbus Junction had seen better days. It was no longer a railroad junction. Main Street was a bit shabby but still boasted a variety of locally owned stores. Judging by the smattering of cars parked in front of them, they seemed to have enough patronage to keep most of them in business. Unfortunately many of the storefronts on street level had been modernized in an ill-advised attempt to prove that they were keeping up to date.

To all of us the focal point in downtown was Carl Lee's barbershop. It was truly a time warp. When you opened the door you entered another world, one that had nothing to do with 1984 and was certainly beyond the experience of most of my young students. We all realized the uniqueness of the place. Aside from photographing Carl and his shop, virtually all of us stopped in for at least one haircut during the time we were there. This quiet old man—he was in his eighties—was still using the original tools he had purchased when he graduated from barber school. With a steady hand he was still giving shaves with an ancient pearl-handled straight razor.

The day we set our clocks back an hour to standard time in the fall of 1984, a colleague of mine stopped at Carl's shop.

Carl was sitting in one of his chairs. My friend asked what he was doing. "Waiting for time to catch up with me. Waiting until it's five again, so I can close up," Carl replied.

Shops like Carl's were once commonplace in almost every American neighborhood, whether Columbus Junction or New York City. Today they are becoming an endangered species, unable to compete with the unisex salons that are proliferating in the malls of America.

Sandra and I stopped at Columbus Junction in September 2003 on one of our numerous trips to Iowa. By now I thought I had become inured to change but not so. I was appalled at what had become of the town I once knew so well. The transformation was so profound that Main Street was unrecognizable. It had undergone a most unfortunate refurbishing, which had obliterated virtually anything I remembered. Like so many Middle Western towns today, its demographics have changed dramatically. The population is now nearly 40 percent Hispanic. As the farming hinterland has become more and more the domain of agribusiness and conglomeration, Columbus Junction has lost its traditional role.

At the end of Main Street I found the old Kent Feed Store, a favorite haunt of my students. It was completely abandoned now and I spent a long time quietly photographing it. At one point an elderly man approached me and asked what I was doing. I explained that I was photographing places that I remembered from the time I ran a workshop here. We made small talk about how time had changed everything. Finally I asked if he knew Carl Lee. Yes. Carl had always cut his hair. He said Carl had closed up his shop a few years ago and had just passed away. "He was a hundred years old."

In March Iowa may have been bitterly cold and windy—but the light! Tornadoes to the south through Missouri and near blizzard conditions to the north combined to make perfect photographic light. It took us all day to cover twenty miles of Webster County west of Fort Dodge. There was so much to photograph that we made Storm Lake well after dark, just before the last place to eat closed. The next day it snowed on and off but once again the light was spectacular. It was late in the day before we crossed over the Missouri at Vermillion, South Dakota, and started south through the high country of northern Nebraska. We drove for miles across the rolling plain, until just as the sun was almost gone, Sandra found an abandoned farmstead. The light was failing so fast that the light meter was of little value but the place was so sadly eloquent that I had to do my best to make a photograph. When I had done all I could, we drove silently on toward Norfolk across an absolutely empty landscape under a golden sky.

Everything changed after we left Norfolk, Nebraska—incidentally, the town where Johnny Carson grew up—and headed south. The light almost stymied us but we found Tarnov, an immense grain elevator and an abandoned Main Street where several Rottweilers who were chained up next to a house never stopped barking while we photographed. Aside from Tarnov we were skunked and by twilight we were driving straight into the blinding sun toward Grand Island at nearly eighty miles an hour on Interstate 80.

Although the light looked as if it would be as flat as the day before, March 30 proved to be far more auspicious. We happened to be at the right place at the right time. The sandhill cranes were migrating—one of nature's truly spectacular events. There were literally tens of thousands of the magnificent birds everywhere as we crossed the Platte River Valley. However, by the time we reached Red Cloud, Willa Cather's childhood home, the light was as dead as a dead mackerel in the moonlight. Photography is straight poker. You play the hand you were dealt or fold. Bad light or not, I had no intention of folding. This part of America had been my turf for years and I had waited a long time to return.

About fifteen miles south of the Kansas line and two miles northwest of the town of Lebanon is one of the most significant points on the map of America. Out in the middle of nowhere on a section road there is a little park. In the park amid a grove of trees is a stone pyramid on which there is a plaque proclaiming that this is "the Geographic Center of the United States." The marker was placed there in 1940, before Alaska and Hawaii became states, so it can only claim to be the center of the *conterminous* lower forty-eight. The town of Lebanon's Hub Club decided to capitalize on its auspicious position. It erected a motel and a restaurant on the site, believing it would be a great tourist attraction and would bring throngs to Lebanon. That was not to be. The location is not only far off the beaten path, it is also happens to be surrounded by a hog farm. Few ever made the trek and shortly after its construction the motel closed. Today only the Stars and Stripes and the Kansas state flag fluttering in the breeze atop the obelisk mark the spot.

We photographed our way south, pausing here and there to explore the possibilities of one ruin after another. Some worked, some proved to be worthless. All in a day's work. At Smith Center we stopped to photograph a beautiful abandoned bank building. As I was waiting for the pigeons to settle down I heard the voice of an elderly man asking me the question I've been asked so many times: "What are you doing?"

"Photographing the old bank across the street."

He hesitated a moment before saying he had been a dentist and had at one time an office on the second floor of the bank. He shook his head and said that when he was in practice it had been a beautiful building. I said something to the effect that I hoped it might be saved. He replied that it was too far gone. The roof was leaking and the upper floors were ready to collapse. "It's a shame. The pigeons have taken over now." He said he hoped to see my book and that a photograph of the bank would be in it. But the light was all wrong and the photograph wasn't any good. The old bank will probably be gone soon without a trace, or a photograph of mine to celebrate its existence.

As the sun was deep in the western sky the light came alive in time to photograph Glade. Nothing but dust on the dusty plain under a pure blue sky. Glade was an abandoned grain elevator next to an abandoned railroad line. The only sign of life was a truck parked next to a tank of nitrogen.

We stopped in Stockton, where we found a mural of a locomotive on the side of a building, which we photographed. I was surprised to find so many murals with a railroad motif: locomotives, depots, passenger trains. Is this not a testament to the importance of the railroads to rural America and how they are missed by those who no longer hear the sound of the train whistle in the night?

We passed over the edge of the Great Plains at twilight before turning in for the night at Hays. It took us another full day to get halfway to Salina because we stopped to explore every town on the way. Once again the light was dead until late in the afternoon. We stopped for lunch at a little café at a crossroads that called itself Gorham. It was just before two o'clock, the time when most small-town restaurants in farming country close. The place was just big enough for four or five square tables. Each was covered with a plastic tablecloth on which were a bowl of sugar packets, a salt and pepper shaker, and a wooden paper napkin holder. Aside from three farmers drinking coffee and joshing with one another at the table in front of one of the windows, the room was empty. A middle-aged woman, who was probably the owner, greeted us with a smile and said to sit anywhere we liked. We took the table next to the window opposite the farmers. She brought us two menus in worn plastic covers. "Coffee?" She filled our cups and we each ordered a grilled cheese sandwich. The sandwiches came in short order on a heavy plate accompanied by two immense pickles and a small pile of chips. She filled our coffee cups again and then busied herself setting the tables for break-fast. In a few minutes she was joined by another woman, who had been doing the cooking in the kitchen at the back of the restaurant. The two of them began to banter with the farmers. We listened and by the time Sandra and I were each brought a piece of real home-baked apple pie and our third cup of coffee, we had learned all the latest gossip in Gorham.

The woman who had been waiting on us asked if we wanted more coffee. She seemed in no hurry, but I realized it was time to go. I asked for the check. The farmers started to get up. There was more good-natured banter between them and the two women, who obviously had known each other for a long time. We said our good-byes. When the door shut behind us, I saw a hand turn the sign over from OPEN to CLOSED.

After lunch we drove on east to the outskirts of Russell, where we stopped to photograph the abandoned Sky Vu Drive-in Theatre. Isn't it remarkable, I thought, that not only one but two U.S. senators, Bob Dole and Arlen Specter, grew up in such an obscure place? But this is America.

As the sun was about to set, we arrived in Wilson, where I had photographed the grain elevators beside the Kansas Pacific's tracks in 1969. It was one of the few places that appeared relatively unchanged, no doubt because the elevators looked like virtual derelicts thirty-six years ago. While I was photographing several people came by and reminded us that many scenes from *Paper Moon,* Peter Bogdanovich's 1973 movie, were filmed in Wilson.

The morning of April 2 started out in Salina. The sky was absolutely cloudless, a sign that didn't bode well for making photographs until evening. We were in for another day of the lifeless light that had plagued us ever since we had left Iowa. I wanted to retrace my steps from a trip I made in 1991, when I was making photographs for *Small Town America.* I was anxious to see how much had changed since then. We headed straight south on Interstate 135 then east across the dead flat country to Gypsum. Everything in this part of the world is dead straight: east, west, north, or south.

Downtown Gypsum was essentially the same as I remember, save that a few more "teeth" had been knocked out of Maple Street as if it had been in a brawl. Where I remembered a row of buildings there was but one left, an old brick drugstore with iron "S" braces along the side that faced an empty lot on the corner of Fifth. Like so many buildings of its vintage, it had the date of construction and, undoubtedly, the name of the original owner emblazoned on the cornice. In this case the date was 1899, but the only letters of the name I could decipher were "S.S." Too many storefront buildings of this kind are either gone or in such deplorable shape that they might as well be torn down. But here in Gypsum there was a glimmer of light. Someone had bought it, more likely rented it, for a song and set up shop. A huge wooden sign with CLASSIC WOODESIGNS on it was displayed on one side of the storefront window and on the other was an assortment of the tools of the trade, including a plane, a saw, and a square.

When I started to write the text for this book, I decided to do a little detective work to find out as much as I could about that old store. I turned to the telephone, as I often do when hunting down information, and called the post office in Gypsum. Karen answered. I explained who I was and what I was doing and asked if she could help me. She went to great lengths to answer my questions and gave me the phone numbers of several people, including Dale Claussen, a former schoolteacher who was now the owner of Classic Woodesigns. He and I had a long and interesting conversation during which he told me that the building had been a drugstore with a doctor's office in the back. No, he didn't own it, but rented it from the Lions Club, which vacated it in 1990. "It may have been a real 'gas eater,' especially this winter. But you should see the interior." He went on to say that there were real parquet marble floors and twelve-foot ceilings covered with pressed tin on the first floor. The Knights of Columbus had occupied the second floor at one time, which was supported by three-by-twelve-foot timbers—"Just as strong as concrete." He paused before saying that "those old buildings, they sure knew how to build them." I asked him whether he had any idea what the name following the initials "S.S." on the cornice was. He didn't. I mentioned the fact that the building was standing by itself and that there must have been other buildings on either side. "There was a movie theater on the south side, but that was gone long before my time."

I told him that I had photographed the bar on the corner in 1991 but couldn't remember the name.

"Sandra Sue's," he replied. "The building used to be part of a lumberyard that took up the whole block. She's selling it."

After I said good-bye, I kept hearing Dale's words ringing in my ears: "They sure knew how to build them."

On the way out of town, Sandra's eye had caught sight of an unpainted abandoned house off to one side of the road. We made a U-turn and drove into the dooryard. We had to pass through an arsenal of bright yellow road construction equipment parked behind the house—an unsettling juxtaposition, for any of those monstrous machines could have reduced the house to kindling in a matter of seconds. But like gorged lions sleeping on the Serengeti they seemed to have no interest in making a kill at the moment. We got out of the car and I walked around slowly for some time trying to find a way to convey the deep sense of sadness I began to feel. It wasn't just an abandoned building. This had been a home, probably to several generations of families. I began to photograph with increasing reverence for what began to be revealed. Impossible, I thought, to try to re-create my feelings through the eyes of a machine. It is one of greatest frustrations of being a photographer, I have found. We were there a very long time and I began to imagine the sounds of happier times. I heard the laughter of phantom boys and girls from other generations playing and the screen door to the kitchen banging open and closed. I imagined I could smell meals being prepared and could see in my mind's eye families sitting down to eat. All sorts of little human dramas passed through my mind. Who were these people? How many generations had slept in the upstairs bedrooms, made love, had children? What did they do? The house was on the very edge of the town. Were they farmers? Perhaps the house had belonged to a man whose name began with "S. S."

I asked Karen if she knew who owned the old house. She didn't, but looked up the number of Dale Faelber, who owned the fleet of construction equipment. I rang him up and explained who I was and why I was calling. Did he own the house? I asked. No. I asked if he knew who did. "A family named Eberhart." Evahard, I heard his wife say in the background. "He died a long time ago and she's in a nursing home. Her daughter lives in Texas. Nobody's lived there for years."

There seemed little else to say. I said good-bye and hung up.

Well, at least I know it wasn't the man with the initials "S. S." who lived there

Later, when I was printing the picture, my assistant, Joe Byrnes, whose family comes from Nebraska, said it was a Sears house just like the one his forebears had lived in.

For a hundred years, from 1893 to 1993, Sears, Roebuck and Co.'s catalog was the purveyor of rural America's necessities. In the early years it included houses like the one in Gypsum. Richard W. Sears, a former railroad station agent, who founded the company and hired Alvah C. Roebuck in 1887 saw the potential of taking advantage of rural free delivery, established in 1896, which allowed catalogs to be delivered to one's doorstep at the rate of one cent per pound. Sears was in every way equal to P. T. Barnum when it came to hyperbole. He proclaimed that Sears was not only the "Cheapest Supply House on Earth," but added that "Our trade reaches around the World." The difference between Barnum and Sears was that Sears was telling the truth.

In short you could order almost anything—a whole farm, for that matter—and have it delivered anywhere. I remember as a boy in Vermont spending hours poring over the pages of the Sears catalog, mesmerized by the variety of goods, most of which, as I remember, were available in three grades: good, better, and best. The Sears catalog was in many ways a mail-order general store, which unlike Wal-mart, Costco, and Home Depot coexisted with the downtown stores rather than driving them out of business.

Once again we headed east on Highway 4 across the line into Dickinson County. A few minutes later we turned into the village of Carlton. The last time I was here I stopped to photograph a large hand-lettered sign on a board by the side of the road as you drove into town, which proclaimed IN 1986 NOTHING HAPPENED HERE.

As far as I could tell nothing had happened since—aside from the fact that the railroad had been torn up, that the old post office and the grocery were abandoned and that there was nothing else on Main Street. The commodious, old Baptist church up on Kentucky Street was still there. I didn't see any indication that there would be a service next Sunday. If there were, I doubt if it would very crowded. According to the 1990 census, Carlton's population was only 39. In 2000 it was 38. As in so many other prairie towns, the only activity centered around the grain elevator. In Carlton's case it consisted of several immense concrete silos down by the defunct railroad right-of-way.

During the several hours we spent photographing in Carlton last spring there was nary a soul to be seen. I was curious to find out about the signs. When I asked Karen at the Gypsum post office about them, she thumbed through the pages of another telephone book and found the number of Patty Schlesener, who works for the rural water district in Carlton. "If anybody can, she should be able to help you."

She did. We spent a most enjoyable half hour on the telephone talking about Carlton and about small towns in general. I asked many questions. I discovered that the sign by the side of the road was painted by Faith Meyer, who lived across the street from them and who was the woman who asked me what I was doing photographing back in 1991. The post office was closed in 1995 and all mail today comes out of Gypsum. Patty confirmed that, as I suspected, there are no services in the Baptist Church (she lives next door).

I asked about the railroad. She said it was torn up about five years ago. "It was tough on the elevator once the trains were gone. They had to get more trucks to haul the grain." She paused.

"It's hard enough as it is for small towns. We're already struggling to maintain ourselves today."

She said she used to listen for trains all night long. "I would always watch them go by in the daytime. Now that they are gone, I sometimes think I still hear them."

I told her that I used to listen for the whistle of the Central Vermont when lying in bed on our farm in Vermont.

We talked about all the changes we had both witnessed— not only about the loss of the railroad but about how Main Street wasn't Main Street anymore. I described Si Davis's general store and Mrs. Mellen's store—more correctly, Mellen's High Grade Meats, Fruits & Vegetables—in Putney. Mellen's was not only a store, it was the town club, like so many similar places in small towns all over America, where in the afternoon men gathered and sat around the stove. I told her that there were three garages in town and that each had its own fiercely loyal customers who wouldn't have thought of patronizing the others.

Patty told me that Laurence Ott, who was Carlton's only mechanic for years, had died recently and that his garage on the west end of town had closed. "There are no restaurants in town so all the men used to gather for coffee at Laurence's after their choring was done. Now that he's gone, they get together at the elevator." She laughed. "We call them the Liars Club. Those men are just as good at gossip as women." She laughed again.

Before we said good-bye Patty told me Faith Meyer had been a painter of landscapes as well as signs. I finally reached Faith and her husband, Virgil, later in the day. Once again, I had to explain who I was and why I was calling, that I had stopped to photograph the sign in 1991. She hadn't a clue who I was but said that she had painted only one sign. I mentioned that Patty had said she was a landscape painter, to which she replied that she was eighty-four and her eyesight was failing so she couldn't paint anything anymore.

And so that is all I know about the sign IN 1986 NOTHING HAPPENED HERE. In 2004 it looked as if nothing would ever happen here again.

It was close to noon when we left Carlton. I had hoped to stop for lunch at Betty's Café in Ramona, a place I remembered with great fondness. I had stumbled into town by accident late one afternoon in May 1991. It was too late to photograph, but not too late to explain to the few people I ran into that I was doing an article on small towns and to say I would be back. When I arrived the following Saturday morning as promised, I noticed that most of the women had their hair up in curlers, no doubt hoping to be looking their best if I should ask them if I might take their portraits.

According to the gazetteer I was using at the time, Ramona claimed to be home to 116 inhabitants. I met 6 of them that day but I don't remember catching a glimpse of the 110 others. Ramona was a mere mite of a town, but a town nonetheless. From all appearances it obviously had seen better days. Main Street had been lined with rows of late-19th- and early-20th-century wooden false-front commercial buildings, which were once indigenous to small-town America. There were enough examples left for me to reconstruct how it might have looked in its heyday. Interestingly, I was to discover after my visit that Ramona's Main Street was used as a classic example in *The Buildings of Main Street: A Guide to American Commercial Architecture,* which had been published by the National Trust for Historic Preservation in 1987.

That warm Saturday in May 1991, when I spent the day photographing Ramona, its Main Street was still very much alive in a somnolent way. Such was not the case last April, when Sandra and I crossed over the railroad tracks and turned onto Main Street. There was no there there. The downtown I remembered didn't exist. Like so many of its counterparts all over rural America, Ramona was one step ahead of being a ghost town. Hanchu's Grocery was no longer; I spent several hours in 1991 talking to Frances and Clinton, who had owned the store for forty-seven years. There was no sign of the two cafés on the other side of the street, Betty's and Sader's, where I had spent the better part of a day. Betty's, which doubled as a bar, also rented videos and you could play all of about half a dozen songs on a vintage jukebox. Betty and her husband, Harold, who owned the café, had come to Ramona in 1952. "Came over here when we got married; been so broke we couldn't leave," she had told me with a laugh. I met Bruno Mauser, a retired merchant seaman, at Betty's. He came up from nearby Tampa every Saturday for a beer or two. I also met Maurice Stroda, who owned the only garage in town, at Betty's. I asked Betty and Bruno if I could take their portraits. Betty has one of the most beautiful faces I'd ever seen and her portrait turned out to be one of the best I've ever made. As the afternoon wore on, Maurice insisted that I visit his establishment. I spent much time photographing the hub caps on the wall of his garage, which featured the warning: NOT RESPONSIBLE FOR ACCIDENTS in huge block letters. Then I took a portrait of him in his grease stained striped bib overalls leaning against a gas pump. Finally, as the day was drawing to a close, I stopped in at Sader's to chat with Hannah, whose hair had been in curlers all morning. The curlers were gone. She was sitting at the end of table with a deck of cards in front of her. "Do you play poker?" she asked.

Last April, when Sandra and I stopped in Ramona, there was no sign of Maurice's garage. It had disappeared completely. I couldn't even find where it had been. And what of Maurice himself? Betty's was gone, too. Where was Betty? I wondered where Bruno, if he were still alive, went to while away a Saturday afternoon sipping a bottle or two of beer. I knew from a telephone conversation with Betty a year after I had spent that lovely Saturday in Ramona that Pete, Hannah's husband, had died. The year after I had played a hand or two of poker with Hannah, she was living in the Golden Age Home in nearby Herington.

The little brick bank, which had been open only for a few hours twice a week, wasn't a bank anymore. There was a pickup parked next to it and signs that someone was in the process of fixing it up. By the look of things, I would say whoever it was had a long way to go.

It was high noon by the time we crossed over the tracks in the other direction, leaving Ramona behind for good. I was deeply saddened by what I had found. Just dust and memories. I was sorry I had come back. I wish I could have remembered it as it was that long ago Saturday in May 1991.

I have never forgotten Ramona and always had a nagging question about what had happened to all those people I knew fourteen years ago. I did some research on the Internet and tracked down Maurice Stroda's telephone number. I called him one morning. He didn't remember who I was but nonetheless he and his wife gave me the answers to many of the questions I asked.

Maurice told me Harold Ohlm, Betty's husband, was dead, but his wife corrected him saying he had been taken to the hospital on Saturday. I asked about Hanchu's Grocery. It was now the Ramona Café, which was owned by a fellow whose name he couldn't remember. It is open only three days: Saturday, Sunday and Monday. Betty's had closed "about three or four" years ago. I told him that when Sandra and I were there in April we had seen some sort of antique establishment where Sader's had been. "Yes," he said, "that's right." He said he thought it was owned by some woman who has another place up in Herington. "Hannah died about four years ago and Pete long before that." I told him I had heard about Pete. Then I asked about Bruno. "Oh, he's not with us. He's been gone a long time now."

I told Maurice I had been unable to find his garage. "Came down with the ice four or five years ago. Only the back is left. The town wants us to take the rest of it down." I heard his wife in the background that they were supposed to have some meeting about it "tonight."

"The brick bank's gone too," he volunteered. "Two girls from California took it over. They try to put out a newsletter— a newspaper."

"From California?" I asked, somewhat surprised.

He explained that they really weren't from California. "Their families are from around here."

I asked him how he was and he said he "still had a lot of miles to go."

Then he told me that the hundred-year-old farmhouse a mile south of town, which had been their home for many years, had burned to the ground the previous spring and that they had been living in town ever since. "We were lucky to get out alive." I heard his wife's voice in the background once again: "The old man smelled smoke and I tried to call the fire department but by then half the house was in flames. The phone wires were melted." She said she told Maurice to get the dog while she drove to town to get the fire department. By the time she returned nothing was left. "It was hard to lose everything. We had no insurance. So we had to start all over again."

During our conversation, which must have lasted a good twenty minutes, Maurice kept saying "I can't place you." I tried in every way to describe myself and the circumstances of my visit. I even told him that he had invited me to come over to his garage and that I had taken a picture of the wall covered with hub caps and mentioned the warning NOT RESPONSIBLE FOR ACCIDENTS stenciled on the wall. He laughed, obviously savoring the fact that I remembered, but I knew he had no idea who I was.

I realized that there was nothing more to say and began to say good-bye. Before he hung up he said, "You be sure to stop by next time you come this way."

After our experience with Ramona, I was almost discouraged enough to call it a day. But the day was only middle-aged and I, ever the explorer, decided to follow the section roads to Lost Springs, a town where I had photographed before. I had hoped to find something, but once again it was just a handful of dust on the prairie. By now it was almost three. We were hungry and tired. The light was terrible. We decided to head for the old railroad junction of Herington for lunch. The only place we could find was a Pizza Hut on the four-lane bypass east of town.

When we left Herington it was the best part of the day—the time when the waning light is at its most beautiful—as rich as chocolate mousse, I used to tell my students—and most frustrating. Unless I happen to be in the right place, I am always driven to distraction trying to find some way to use this precious light before it fails altogether. This evening was no exception. We drove across Township 8 into Burdick. Nothing. Then north through Township 7 to Delavan. Still nothing. We turned east on US 56. About an hour of light left. A perfect evening, but nary a thing to photograph. Damn! I finally decided it was time to pack it in for the day and called the Ramada Inn in Emporia to make a reservation. We drove on into Township 9 at seventy mph for seven miles when I saw a sign on the left, WILSEY 1 MILE. I kept on going. I had second thoughts. "Should we check it out?" I asked Sandra. I knew her answer before she replied and so we drove into Wilsey at sundown. The light was failing fast. It was now or never. We looked around. The town was obviously in its death throes. The railroad had been torn up. There was a rather moribund looking grain elevator beside where the tracks had been. There were a few houses on the back street: some abandoned, a few still occupied. I saw a dog behind a fence. As far as I could tell the only establishment in business on Fifth Street—the main drag—was the Wilsey Market and Beauty Shop. Parked in front of it were a van and a pick up truck. It wasn't a photograph but across the street was a very small, interesting-looking building that someone had attempted to refurbish. It had been abandoned, as were all other the buildings on that side of the street, but whoever owned it had planted a line of flowers on either side of the door.

By the time I had set up my tripod in the middle of street the shadows had already begun to creep across the face of the little building. At high noon, time seems frozen, but at this moment, as the sun is setting and it is possible to sense the world turning, one realizes how precious time really is. I watched as time ran out until there was no chance to photograph. Photography is like fishing. You know when you have a photograph, just the way you do when you have a fish on the line. Like fishing you don't always bring it to the net. Wilsey was one that got away. Par for the course I said as I packed up my gear. In my experience 90 percent or more of what you see eludes capture. It's all part of the challenge that has kept me on the road for fifty years.

As we were ready to go the couple who owned the grocery store, Maurice and Evelyn Lee, came out and introduced themselves. We stayed in the street talking about Wilsey. I mentioned that the railroad was torn up. "Oh, yes," Evelyn said. "The Missouri Pacific laid down welded rail. A few years later the Union Pacific took over and they ripped up the new rail and tore up the line through Wilsey. I suppose they used the new rail someplace else." She observed that it seemed kind of stupid to spend all that money and then turn around and abandon it.

There was not much else to tell about Wilsey, except that the "old duffers club" met at the store every morning. I pictured a knot of three or four old men with nothing better to do sitting and reminiscing about the way it was when Wilsey was on the Missouri Pacific's "High Iron" to Colorado and when Fifth Street was lined on both sides with one sort of store or another.

It was full twilight by the time we were back on Highway 56. We turned south at Council Grove, where the Santa Fe Trail began, and headed across the Flint Hills toward Emporia. The Flint Hills are a unique landform, by far the largest tract of tallgrass prairie left in North America. They were left intact because no farmer wanted to break his plowshare trying to subdue the flinty ground. The old "plowmeister" himself, John Deere, the blacksmith from Vermont, knew a bit about trying to deal with rock-bound fields. His cast steel plow with its polished moldboard, which did so much to transform the prairie into America's breadbasket, was of no use here. In the deepening light the Flint Hills looked as if they should have been much farther west, beyond Salina, a piece of the Great Plains transplanted. They gave the illusion of being pristine, but of course they were not. This was once the domain of herds of elk and bison who did not overgraze the land, as do the thousands of heads of beef cattle that roam over the grasslands today. Unless a balance is reached between the rancher and those who believe this great resource should be saved, the Flint Hills—and all the West—may well be reduced to what was once called the Great American Desert.

It was well after dark before we finally reached the outskirts of Emporia. We never found Emporia. What we found was profound culture shock. Emporia was lost in a quagmire of hype and chaos. The Ramada Inn was located somewhere on the interstate amid every conceivable form of garish plastic, screaming lights, and logos. They were all there: McDonald's, Taco Bell, Jiffy Lube, Burger King, Best Western, Pizza Hut. Having spent the day in another world, far from the cacophony of modern-day America, the arrival in Emporia was almost impossible to digest. I wanted to make a U-turn, drive back into the Flint Hills, turn the clock back to 1991, and have dinner at Betty's in Ramona.

Or wind it even further back to October 1968—the day after my birthday, to be exact. It was my first time in Emporia and I was very sick. I needed a doctor so I went to a drugstore and told the pharmacist my plight. He gave me the name of a physician and I went to his office. I waited in a tiny, crowded room. Soon a kindly old country doctor examined me. Bronchitis was his diagnosis. He gave me a prescription for erythromycin. When I asked his secretary what the charges were she said there were none. The office was happy to help out a young traveler from back east. I went back to the pharmacist, who gave me ten capsules of the medicine in a flat cardboard box. Knowing the outrageous fees that most doctors charge today I still can't quite believe this is a true story. But it is.

America is not the country I knew and so greatly admired as a young man. It was far more human then, a country of communities and Main Streets and family farms and most of all the honest work and spirit of the American people, who strove to build a better world. It was largely unpretentious, not often spectacular or of particular historic significance. It was also a far more interesting and exciting place to me than it is today.

For fifty years I have tried to photograph this America we are losing. In every way possible I have said that what we took for granted was disappearing. I realized it would be gone. I was right. It is.

Each time I set forth to photograph, I discovered that something was always different from the way it had been on a previous trip. At first the changes were in slow motion, imperceptible except to the discerning eye: a store on Main Street that had been there the year before was shuttered, another railroad station was abandoned, another farm gone, a factory gone dark. When I began to be concerned about what I saw happening, the interstate highway system was just beginning to scar and tear through the farmland. The time of the mall was not yet in full bloom. People still went downtown to shop, albeit in ever diminishing numbers. There were enough small farms in the hinterland to keep a few local feed mills in business. The factories were still humming. We made things in America then. No longer. For fifty years I have tried to photograph this America before it is lost forever. I realized it would soon be gone. Today the transformation of our culture—change itself—has become the subject of my photographs.

A hundred years from now people looking at my pictures will see an America that no longer exists; a foreign country as different as we today perceive the country before the Civil War.

When describing my work I have always said that I have been one step ahead of the wrecking ball. I have often managed to arrive on the scene with my camera at the eleventh hour. Today the metaphorical wrecking ball has done its work. Far too many places I once knew are now but a handful of dust.

What are the roots that clutch, what branches grow

Out of this stony rubbish? Son of man,

You cannot say, or guess, for you know only

A heap of broken images, where the sun beats,

And the dead tree gives no shelter, the cricket no relief,

And the dry stone no sound of water. Only

There is shadow under this red rock,

(Come in under the shadow of this red rock),

And I will show you something different from either

Your shadow at morning striding behind you

Or your shadow at evening rising to meet you;

I will show you fear in a handful of dust.

—T. S. Eliot, "The Waste Land"

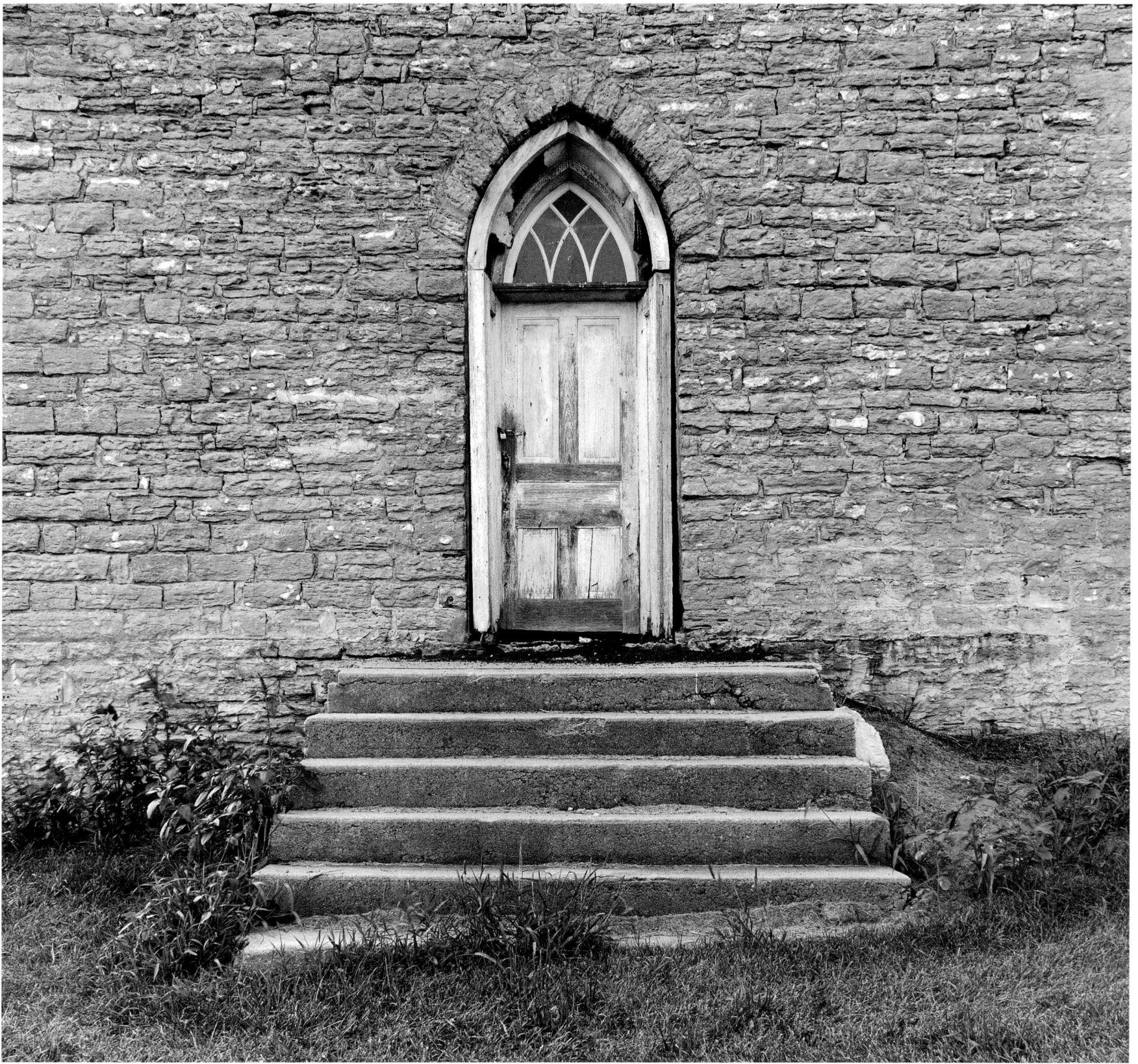

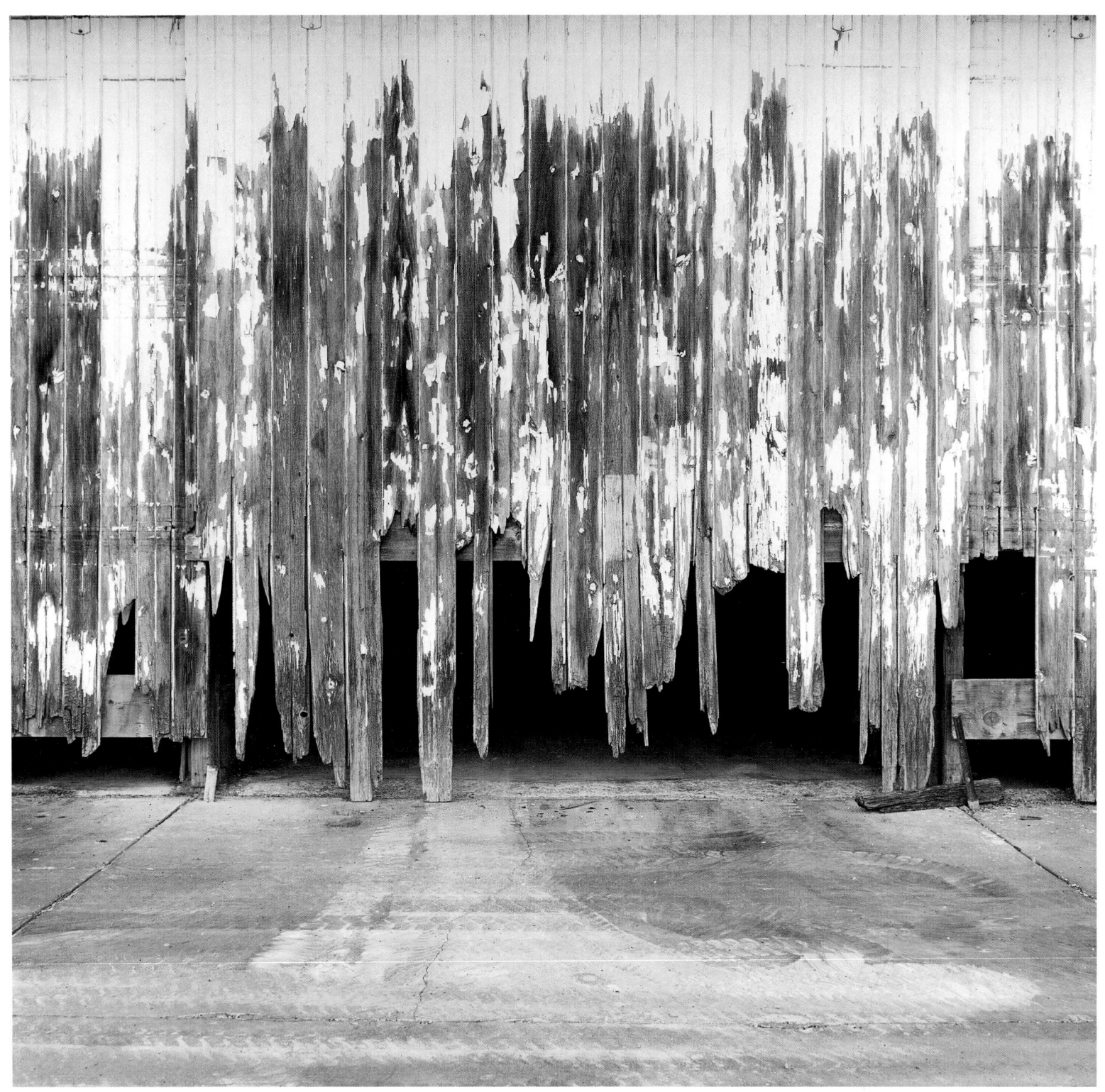

2 · Abandoned Feed Mill, Norway, Iowa (2004) / 3 · Logan County, Illinois (1973)

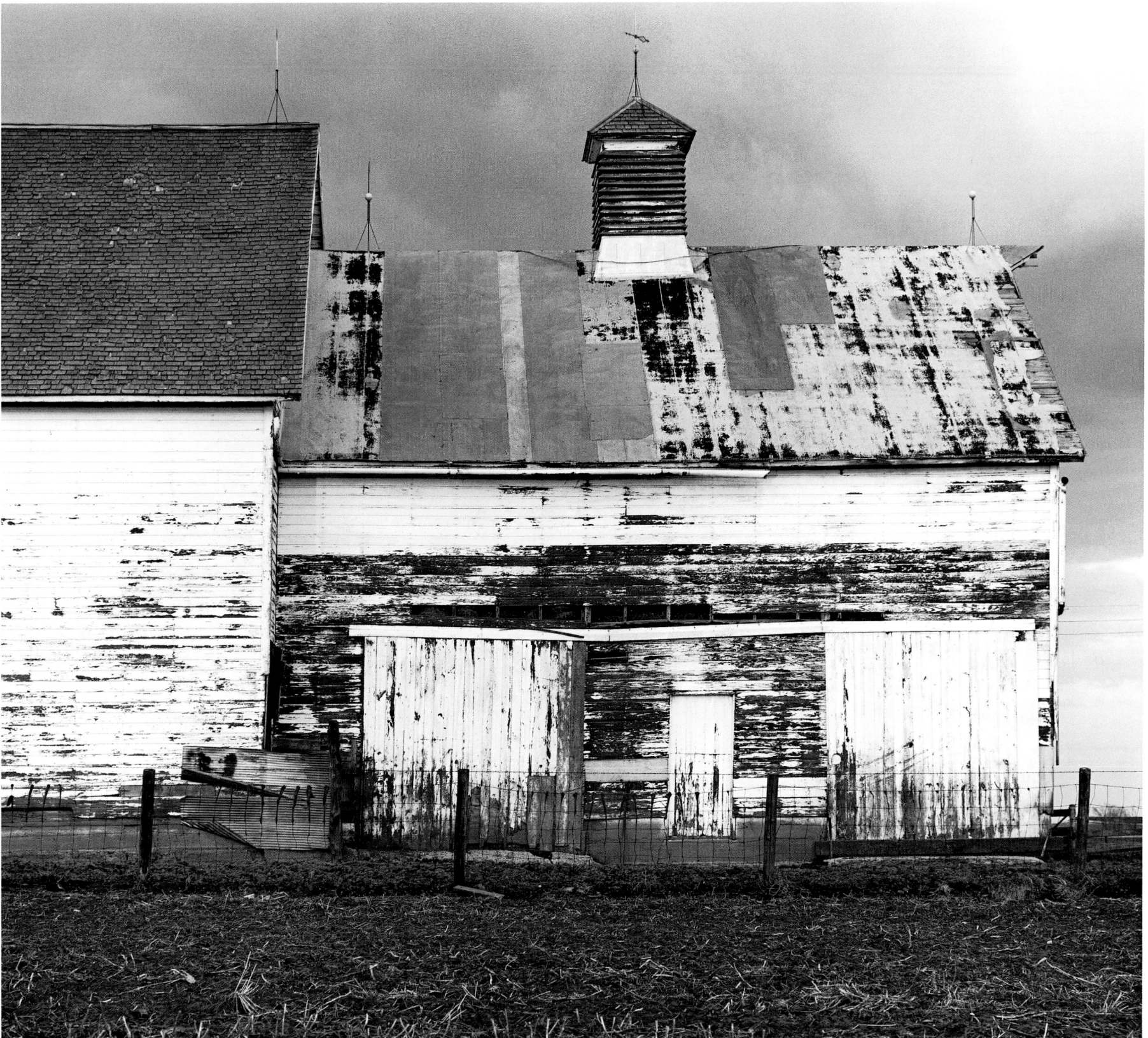

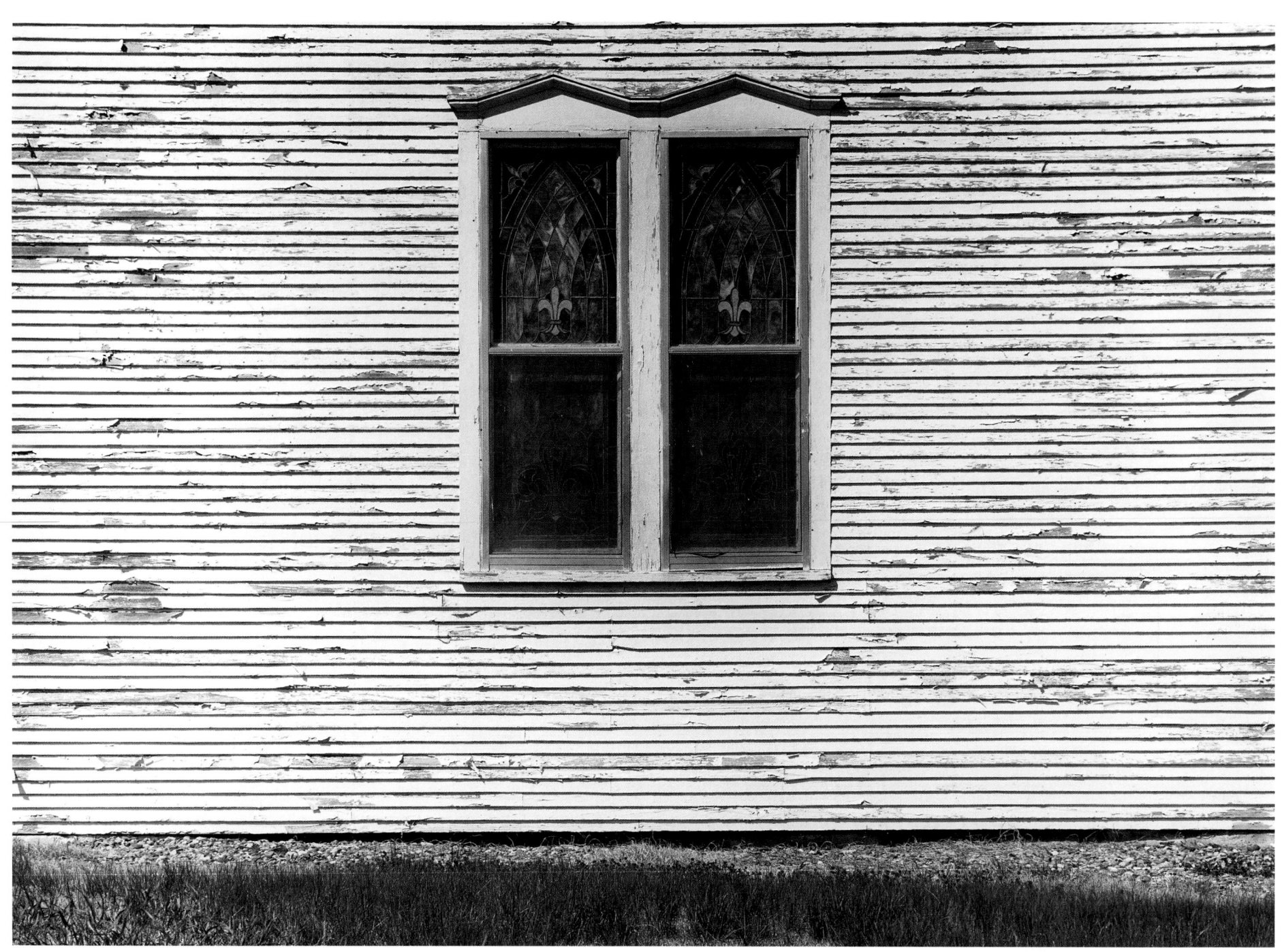

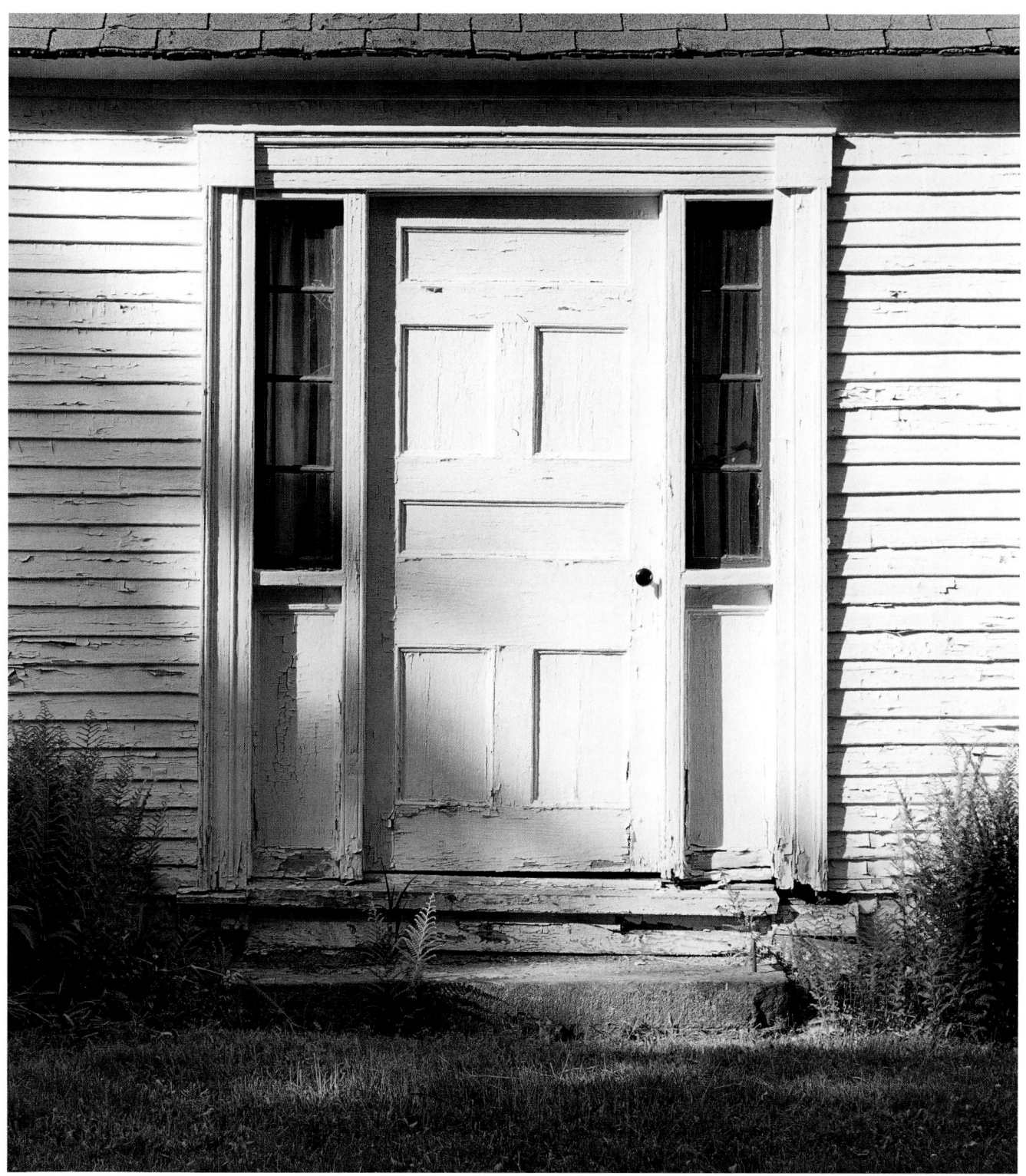

5 · Belknap County, New Hampshire (1999)

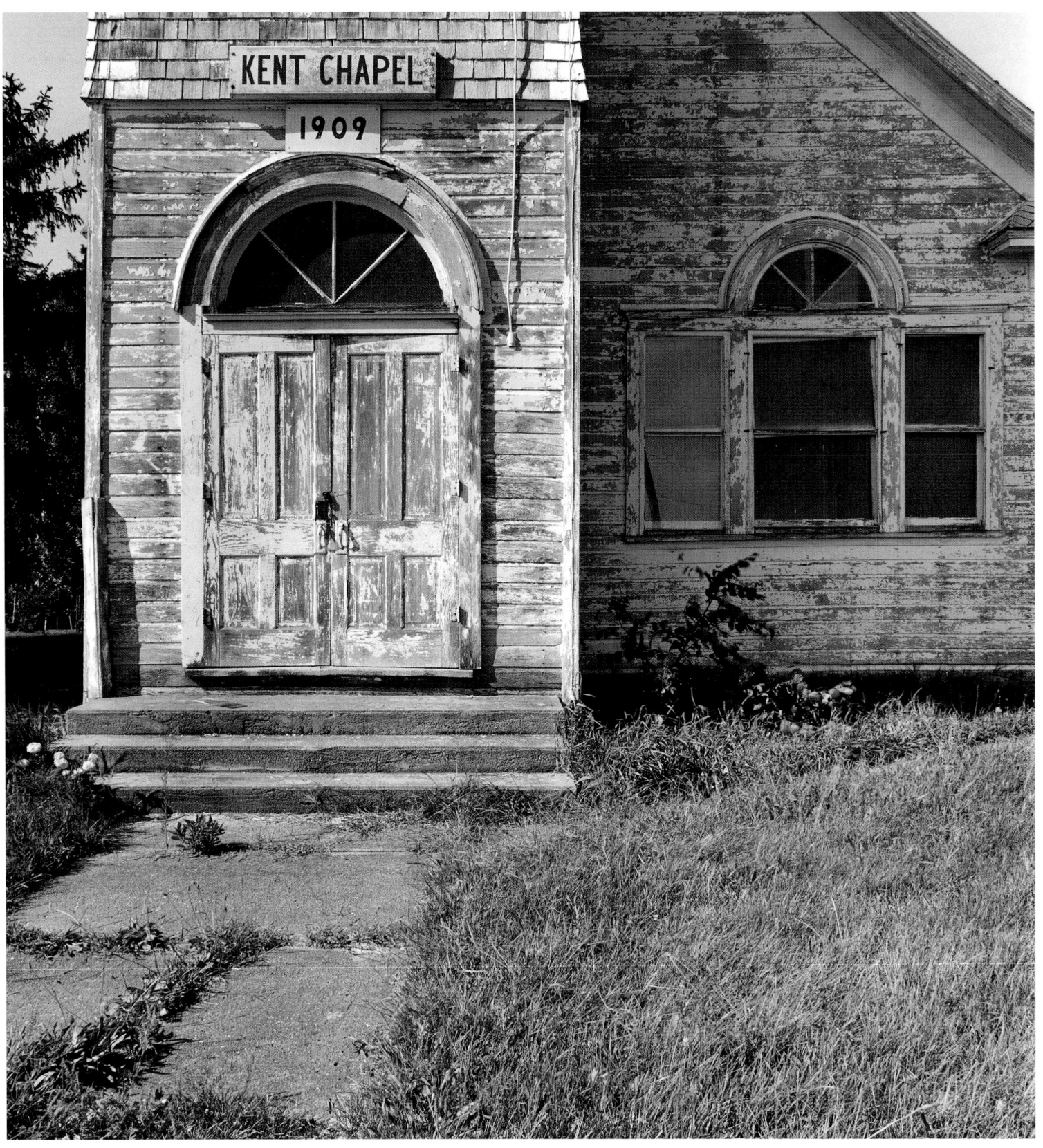

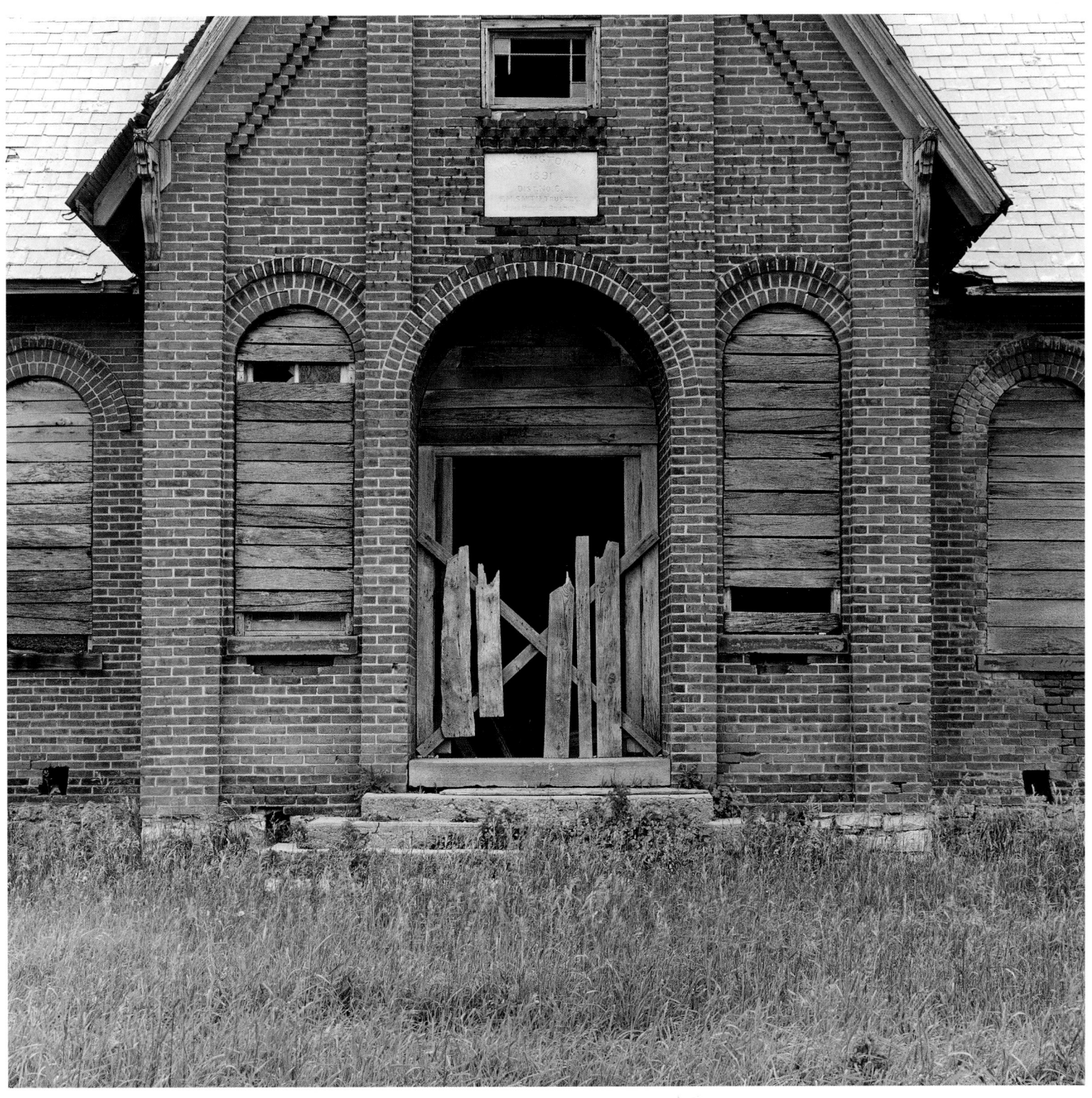

6 · Kent Chapel, Poweshiek County, Iowa (2004)   /   7 · Derelict Schoolhouse, Whitley County, Indiana (2003)

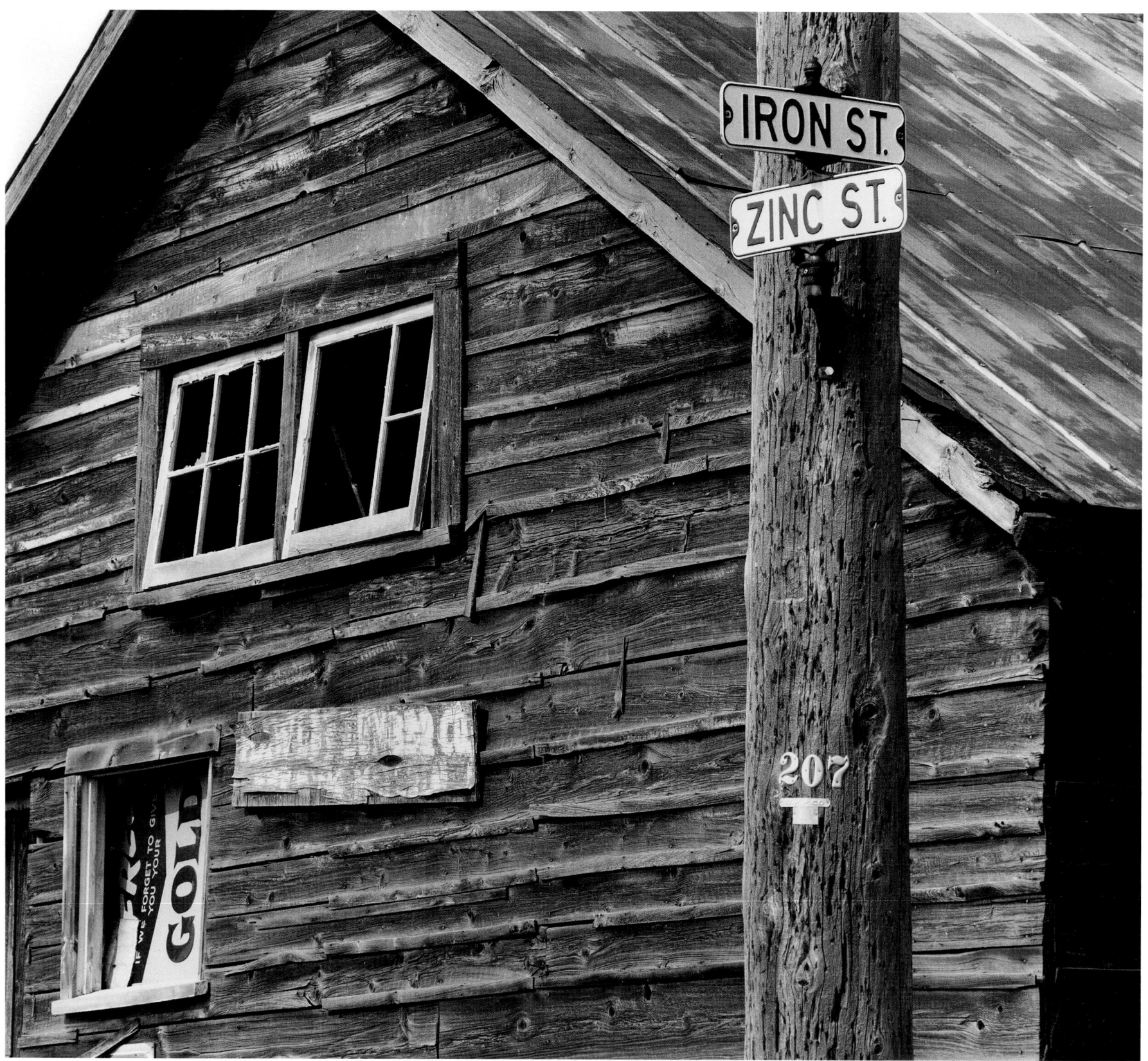

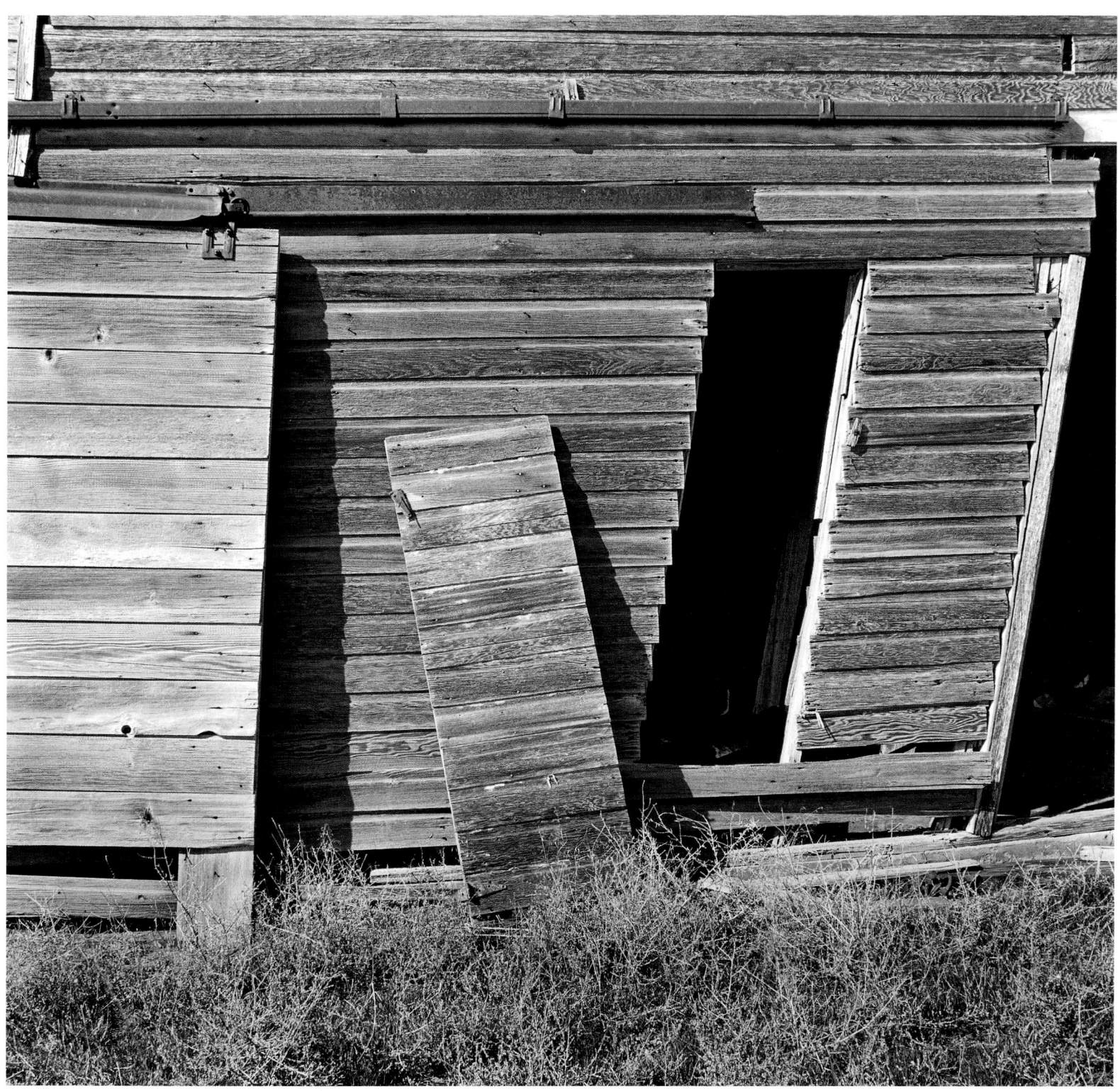

8 · Ontonagon, Michigan (1985)   /   9 · Abandoned Barn, Smith County, Kansas (2004)

10 · Barn Door Detail, Fulton County, Ohio (2000)

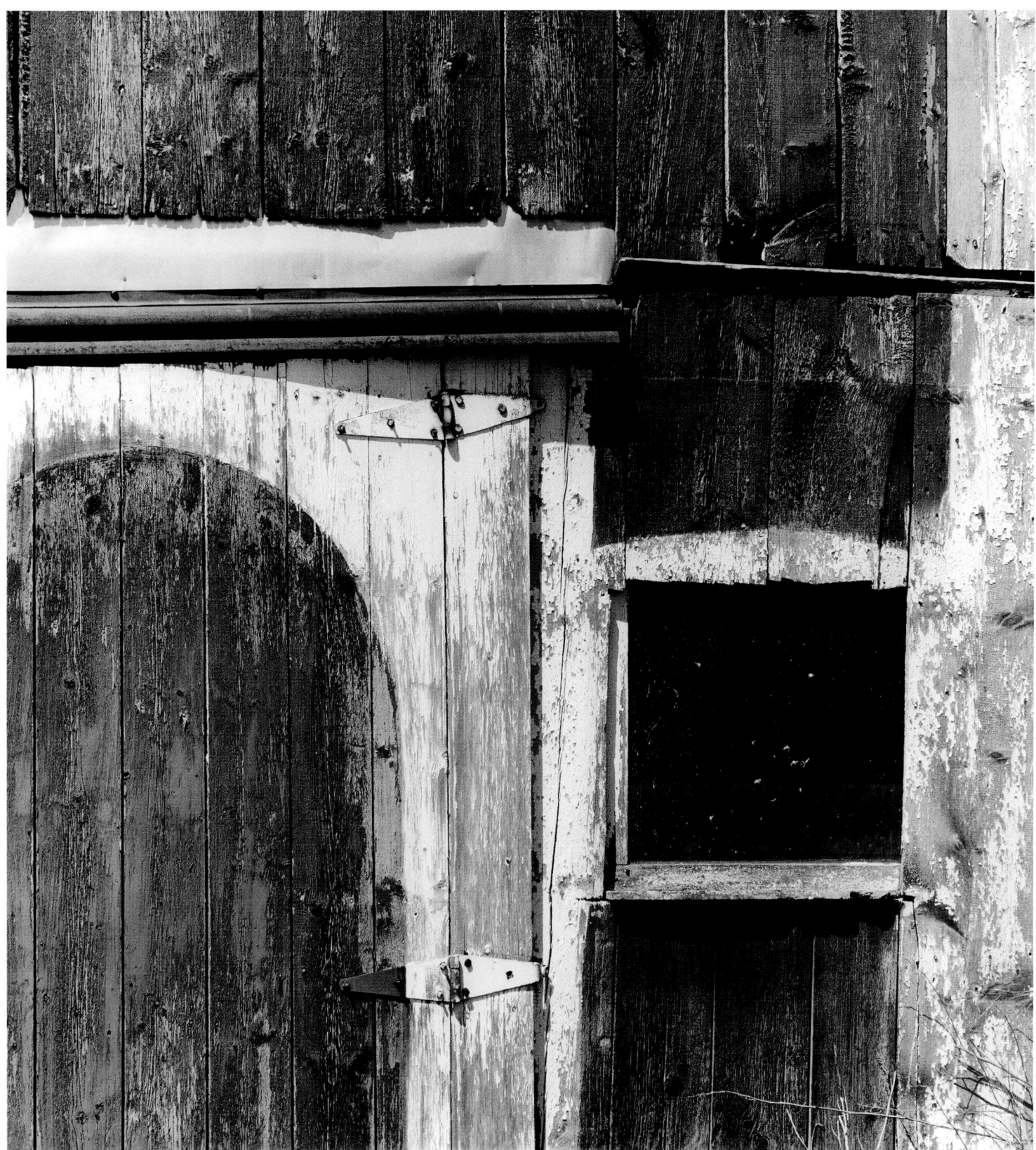

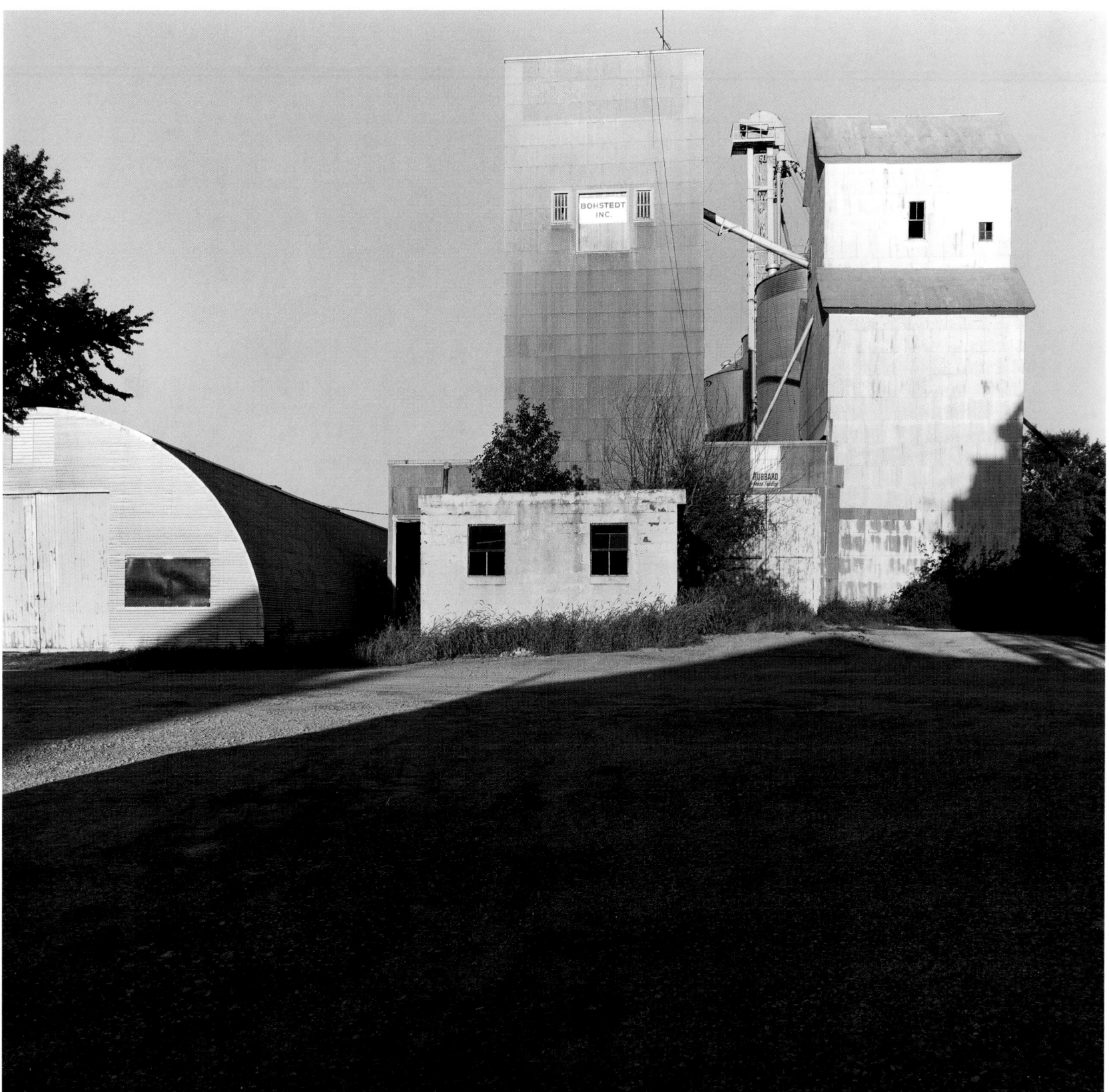

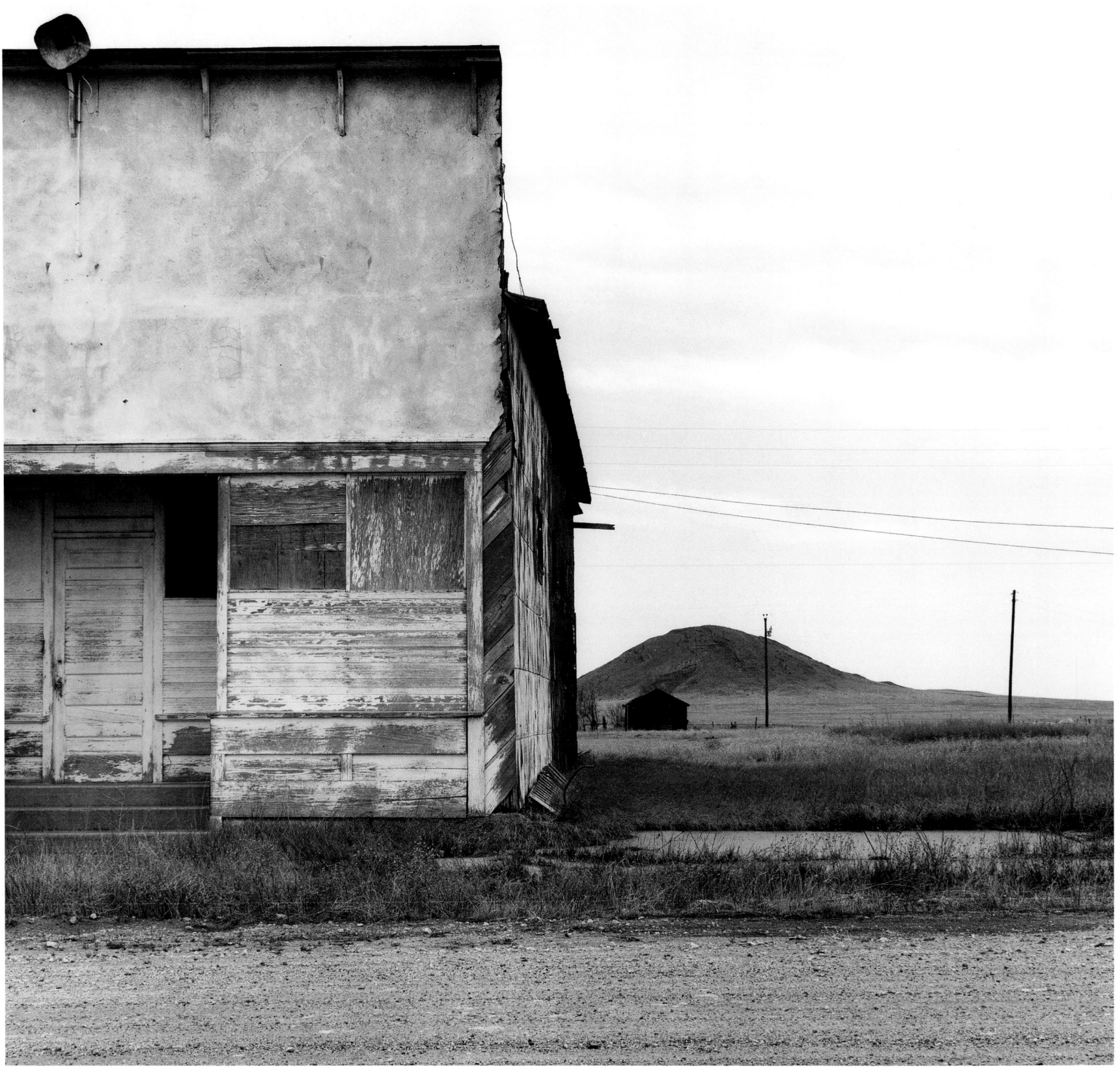

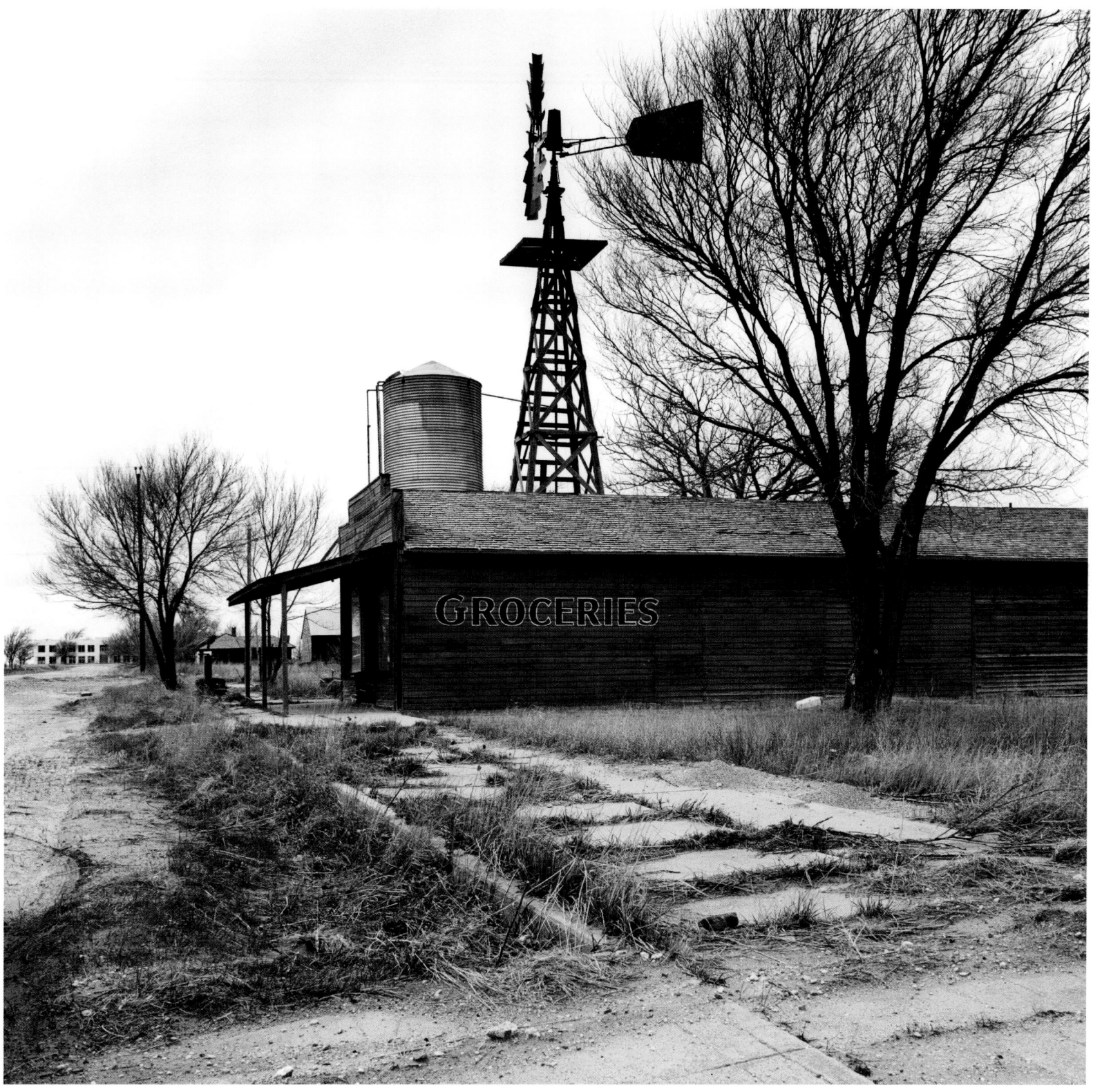

12 · Grenville, New Mexico (1971) / 13 · Grenville, New Mexico (1971)

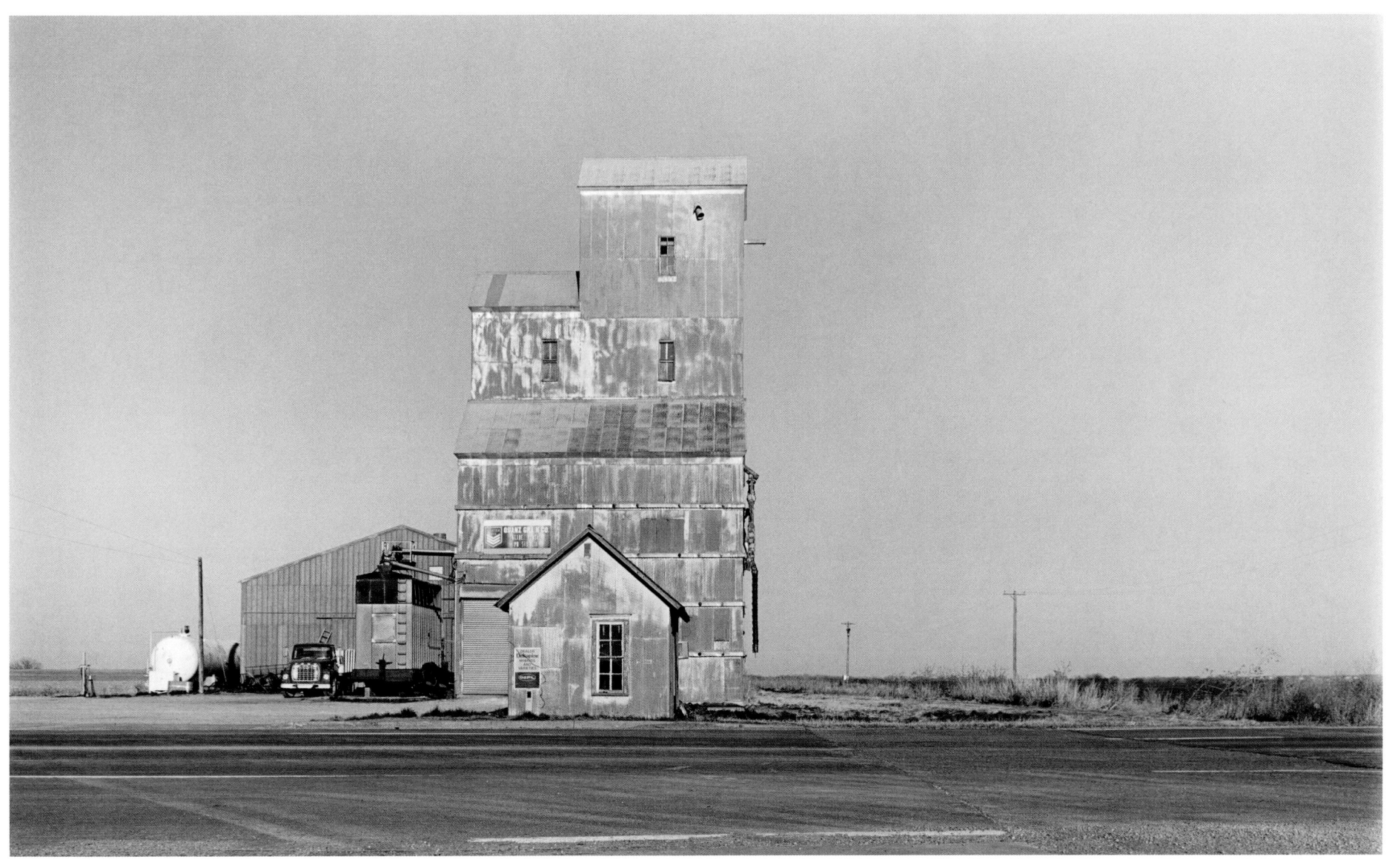

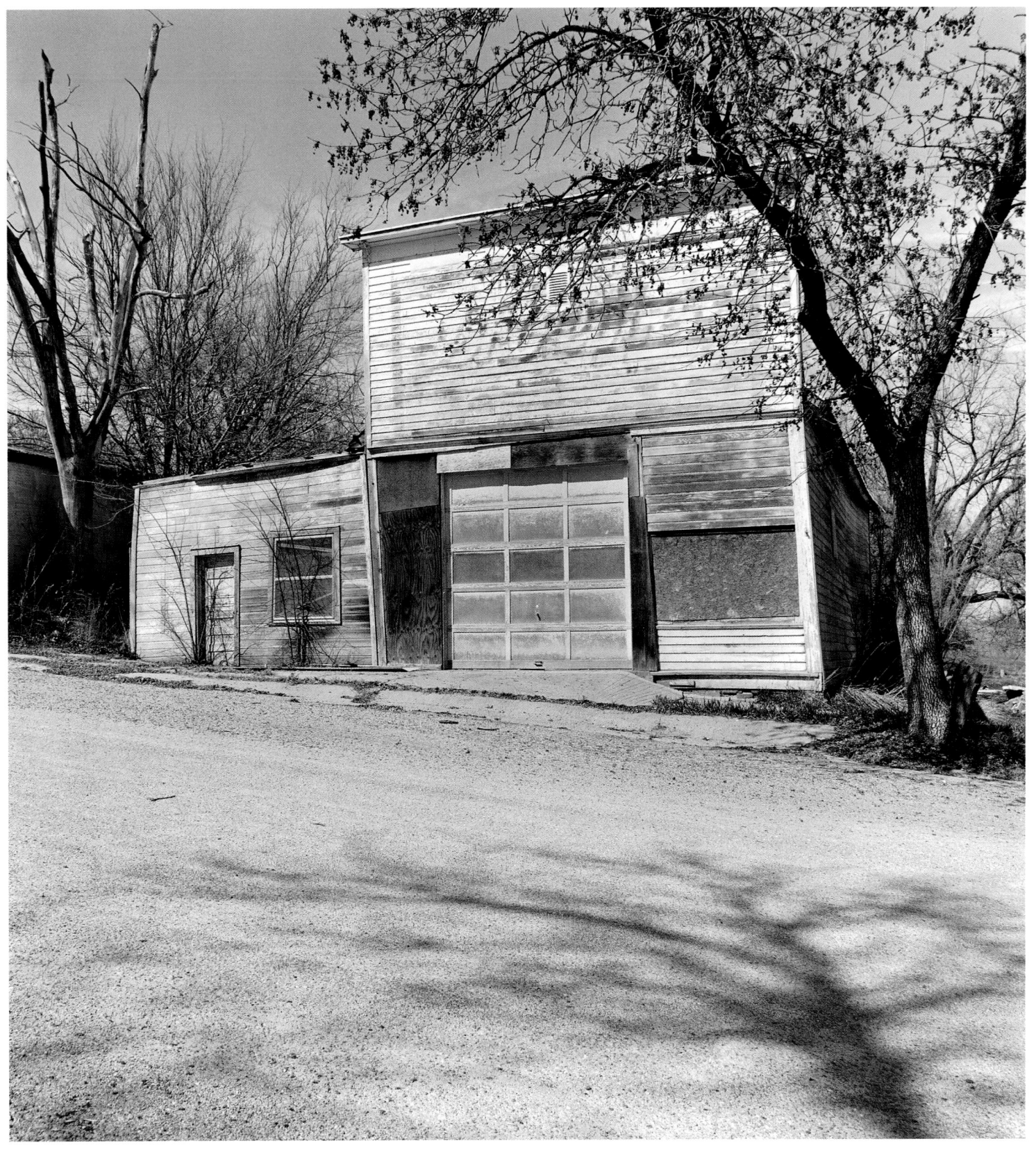

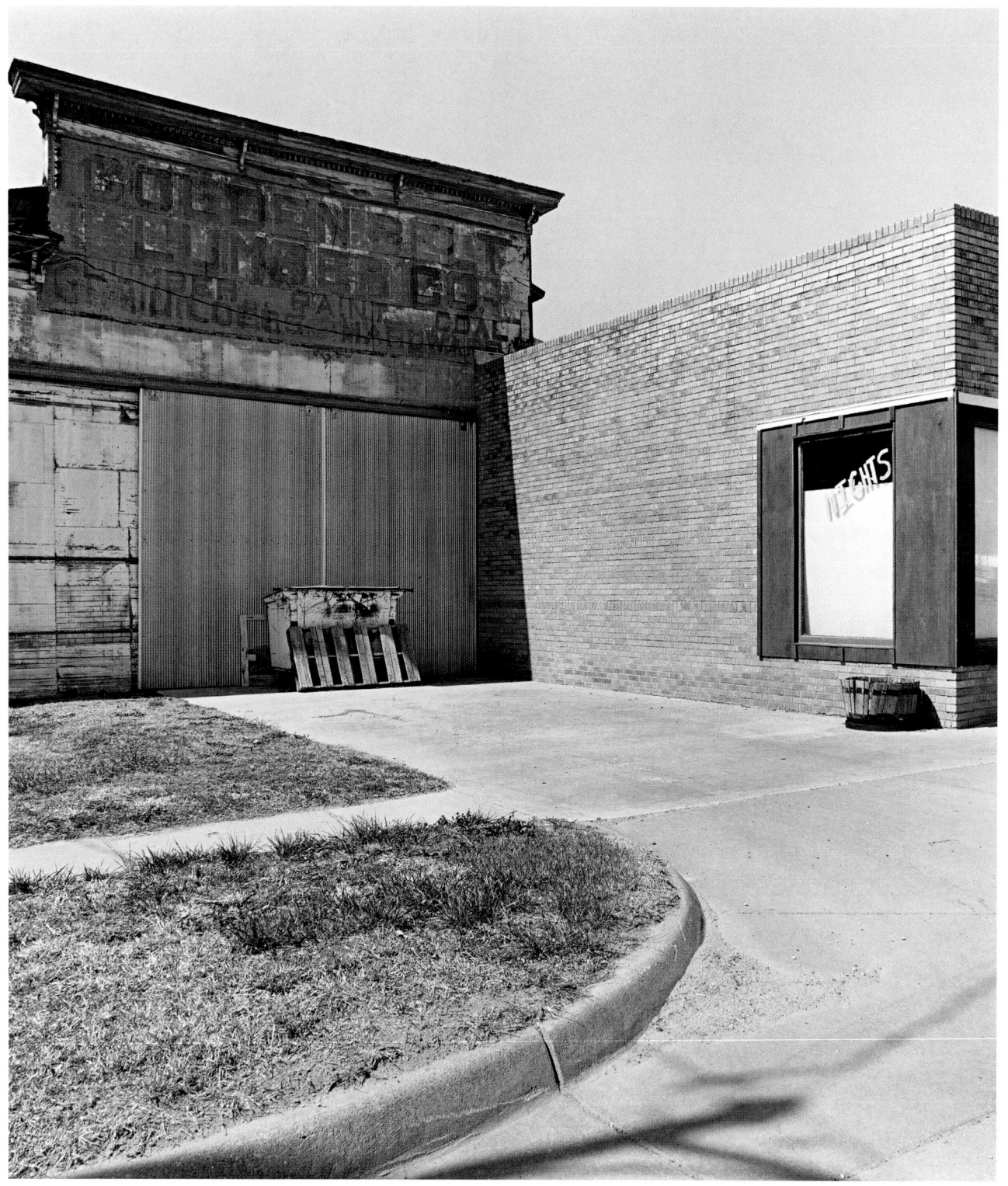

16 · Victoria, Kansas (2004)   /   17 · Wellman, Iowa (2004)

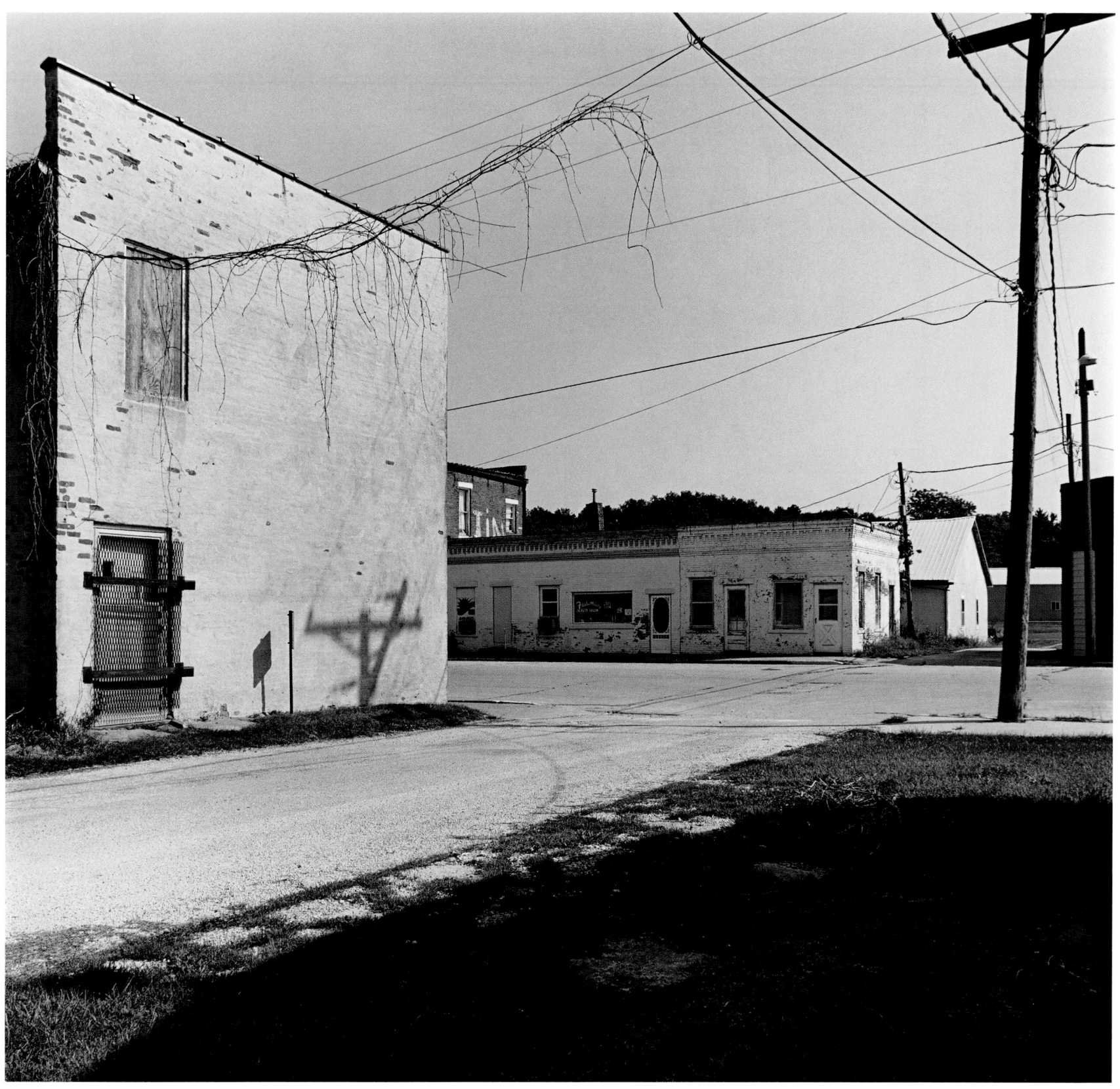

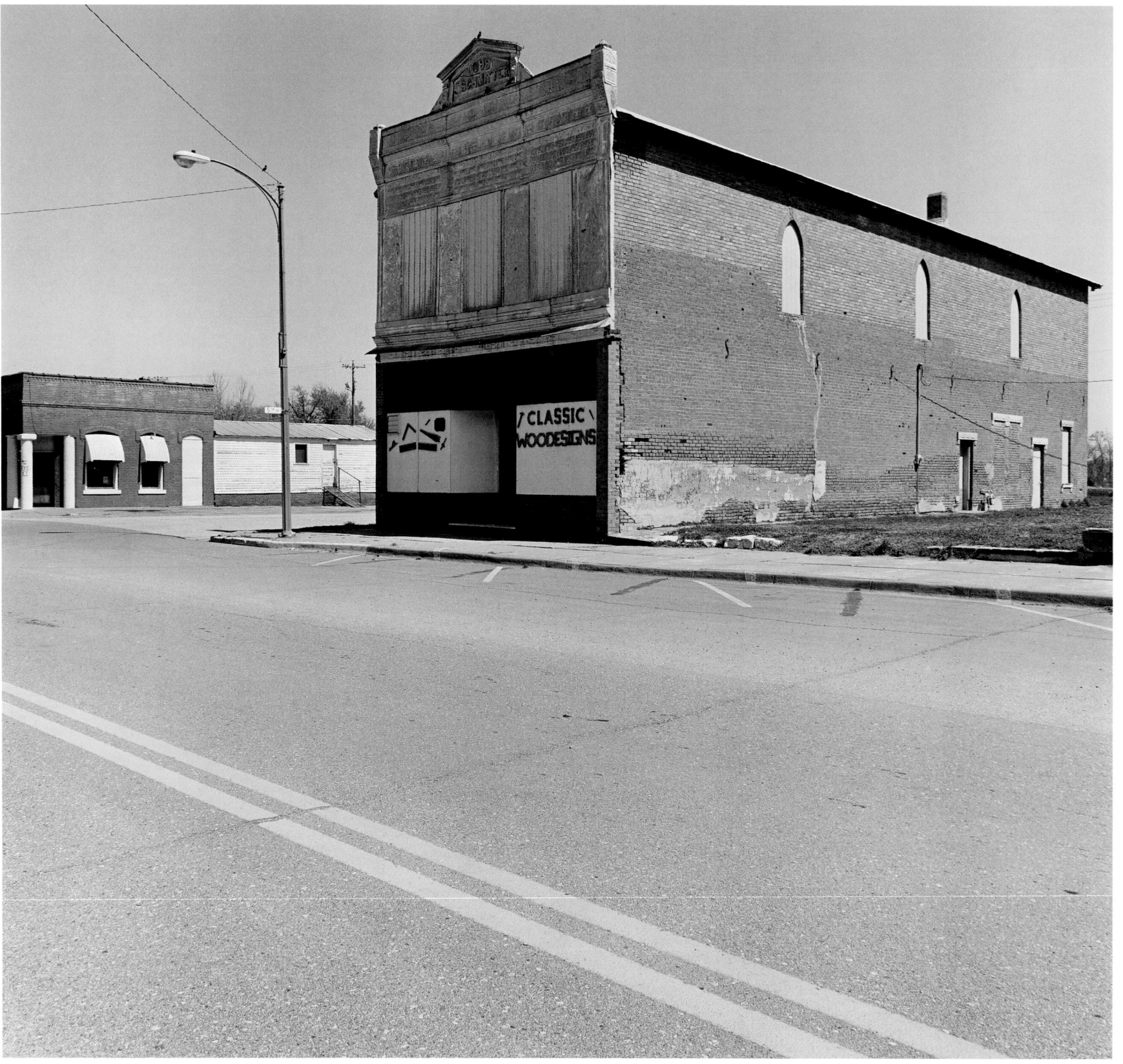

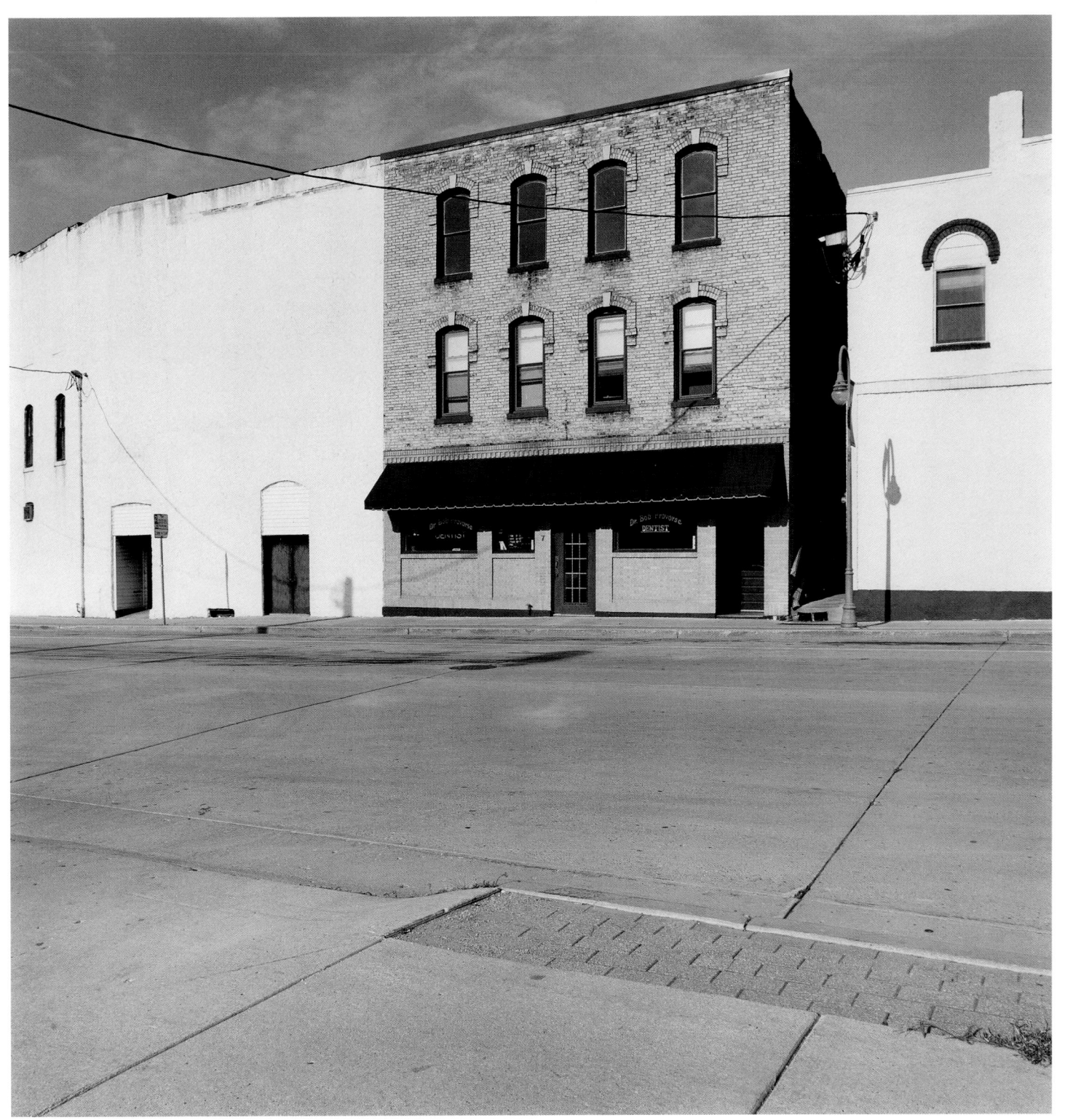

18 · Gypsum, Kansas (2004)   /   19 · Whitewater, Wisconsin (2003)

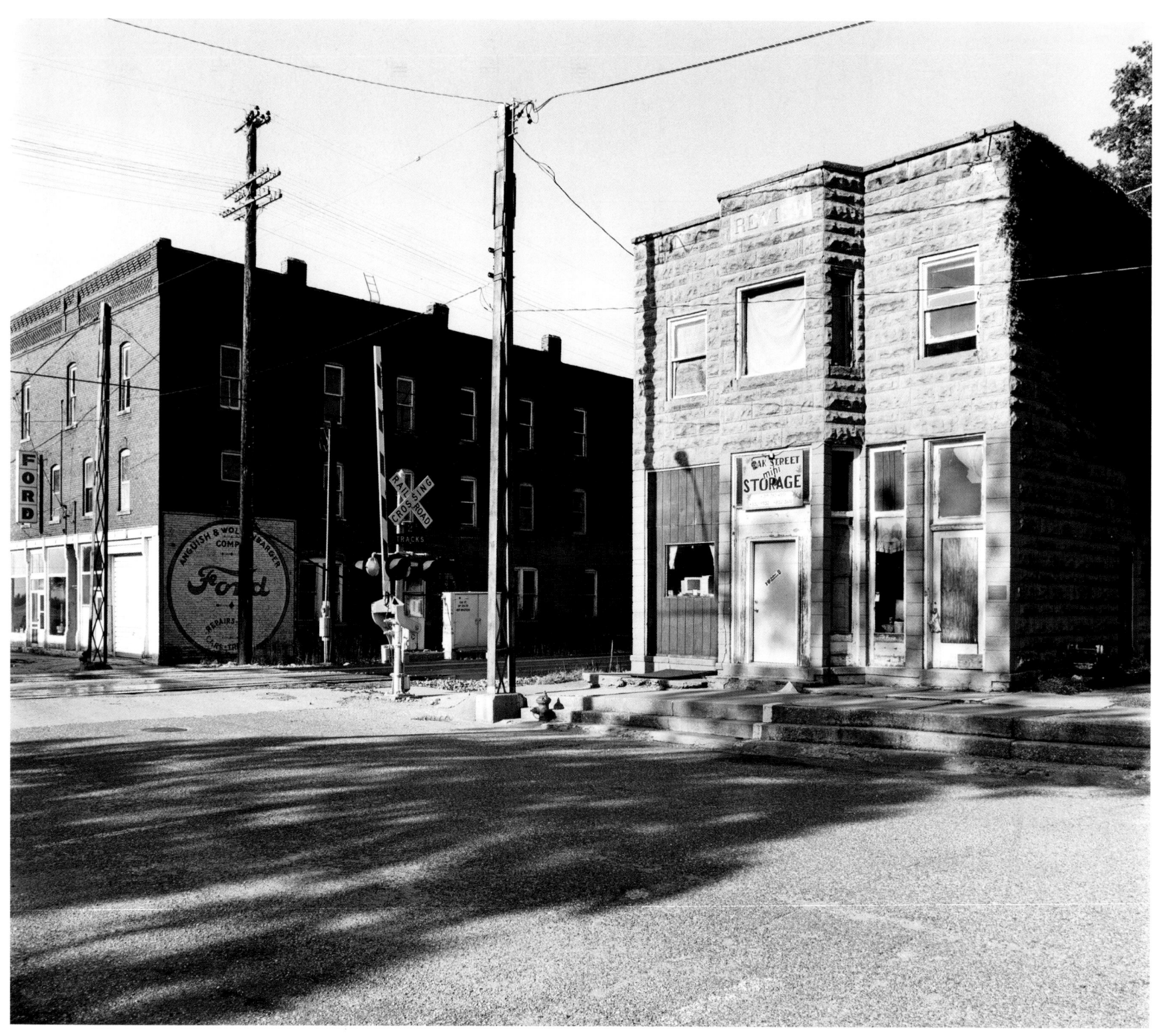

20 · Dallas City, Illinois (2003) / 21 · Klinkert House, Sturtevant, Wisconsin (2003)

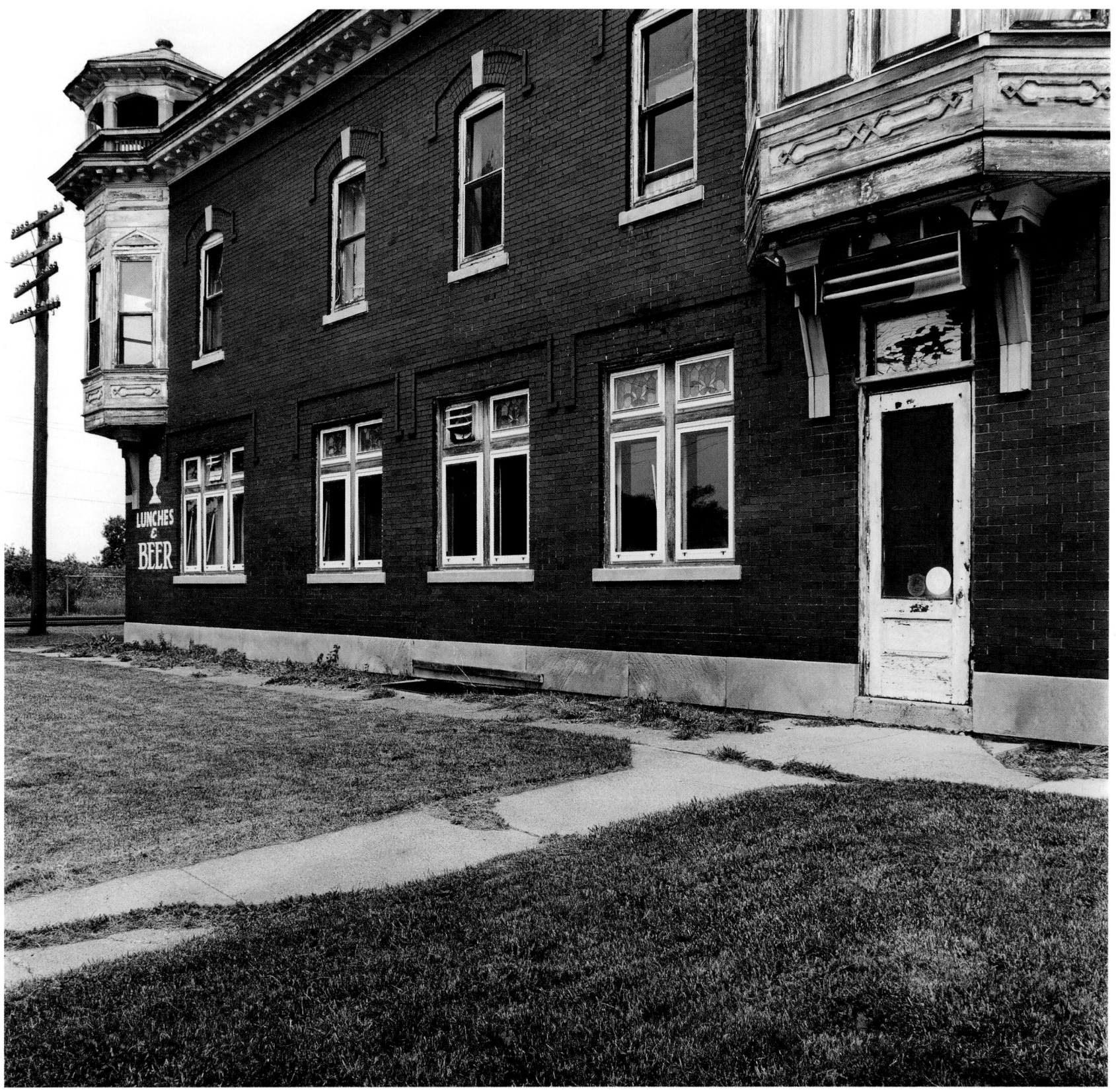

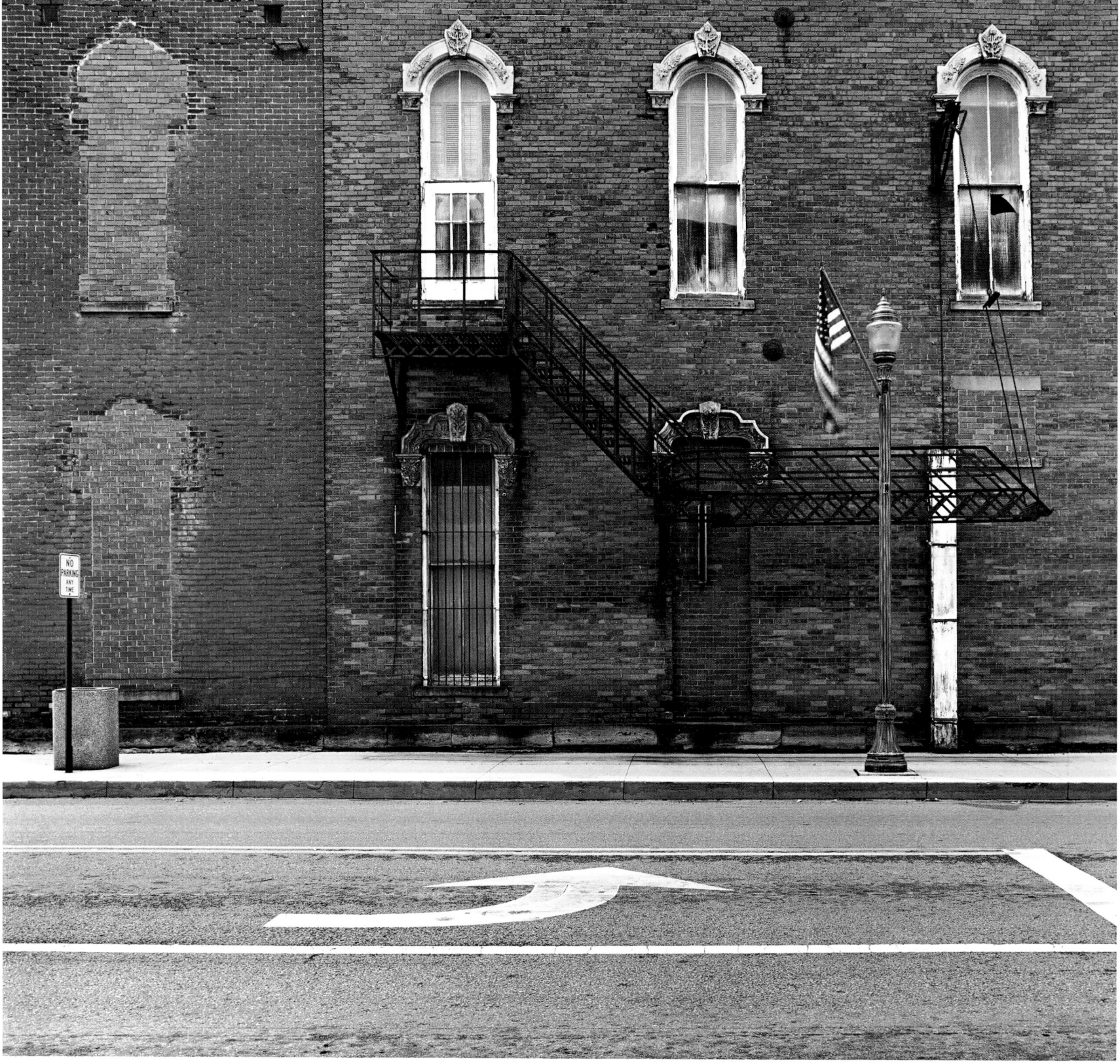

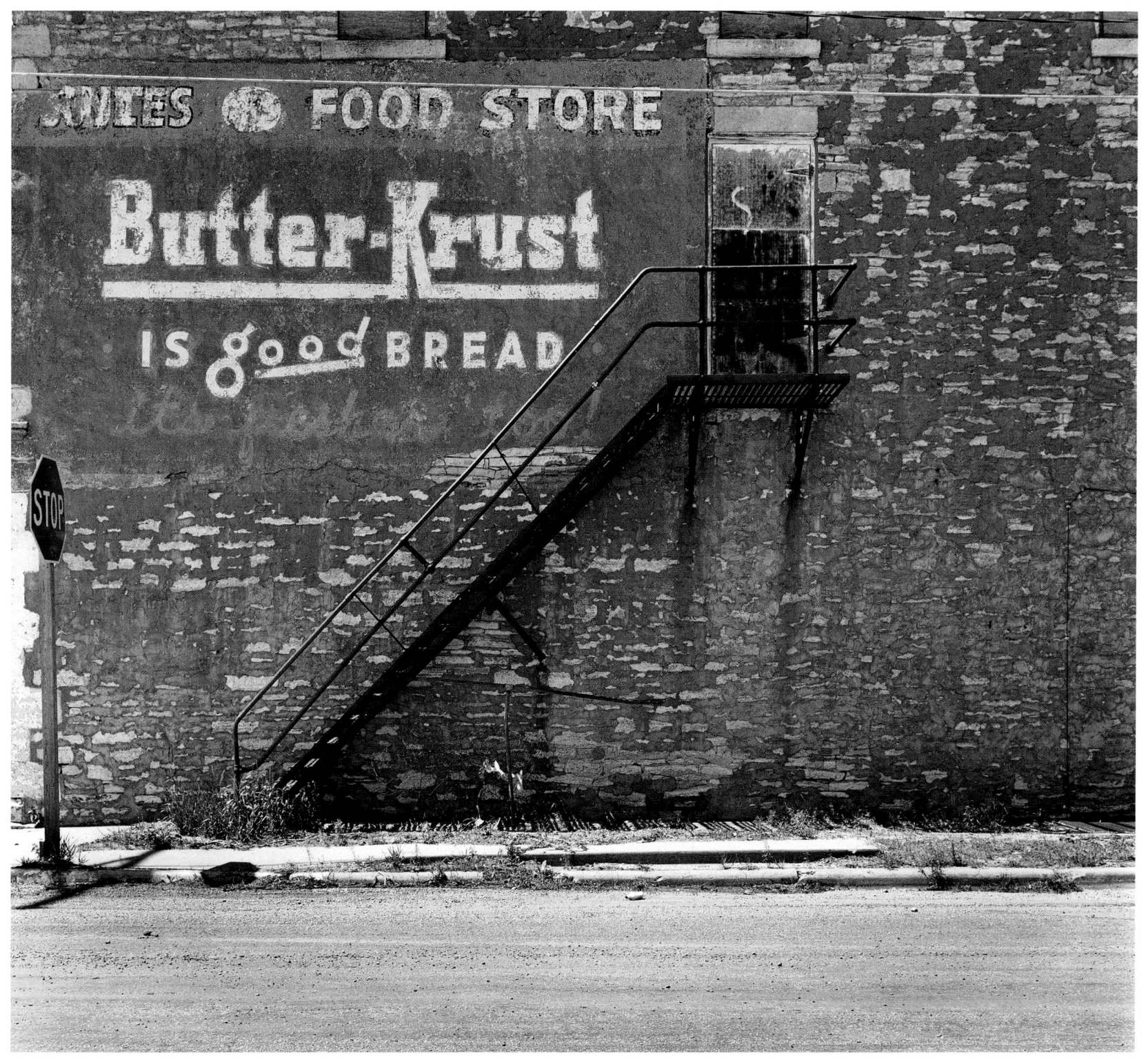

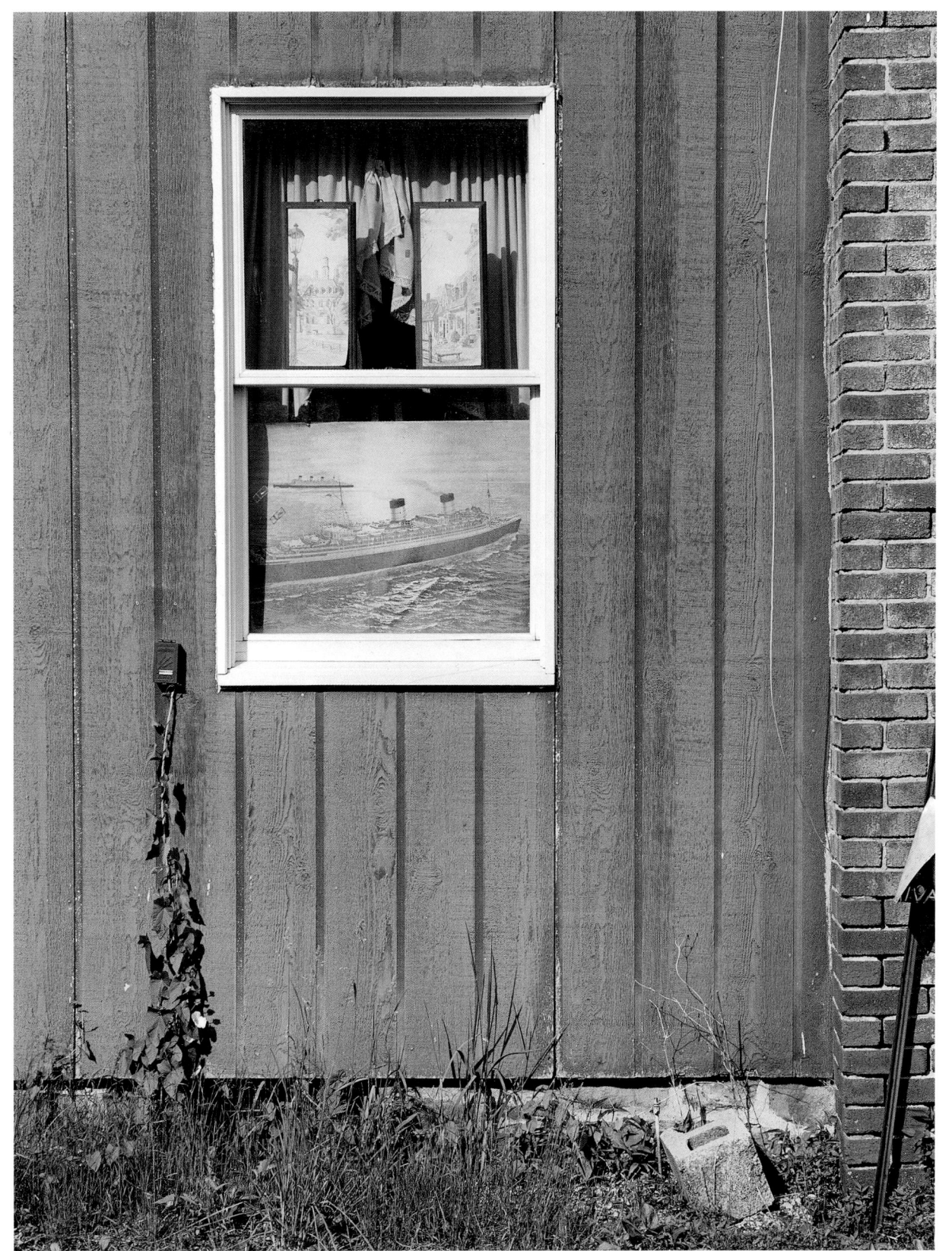

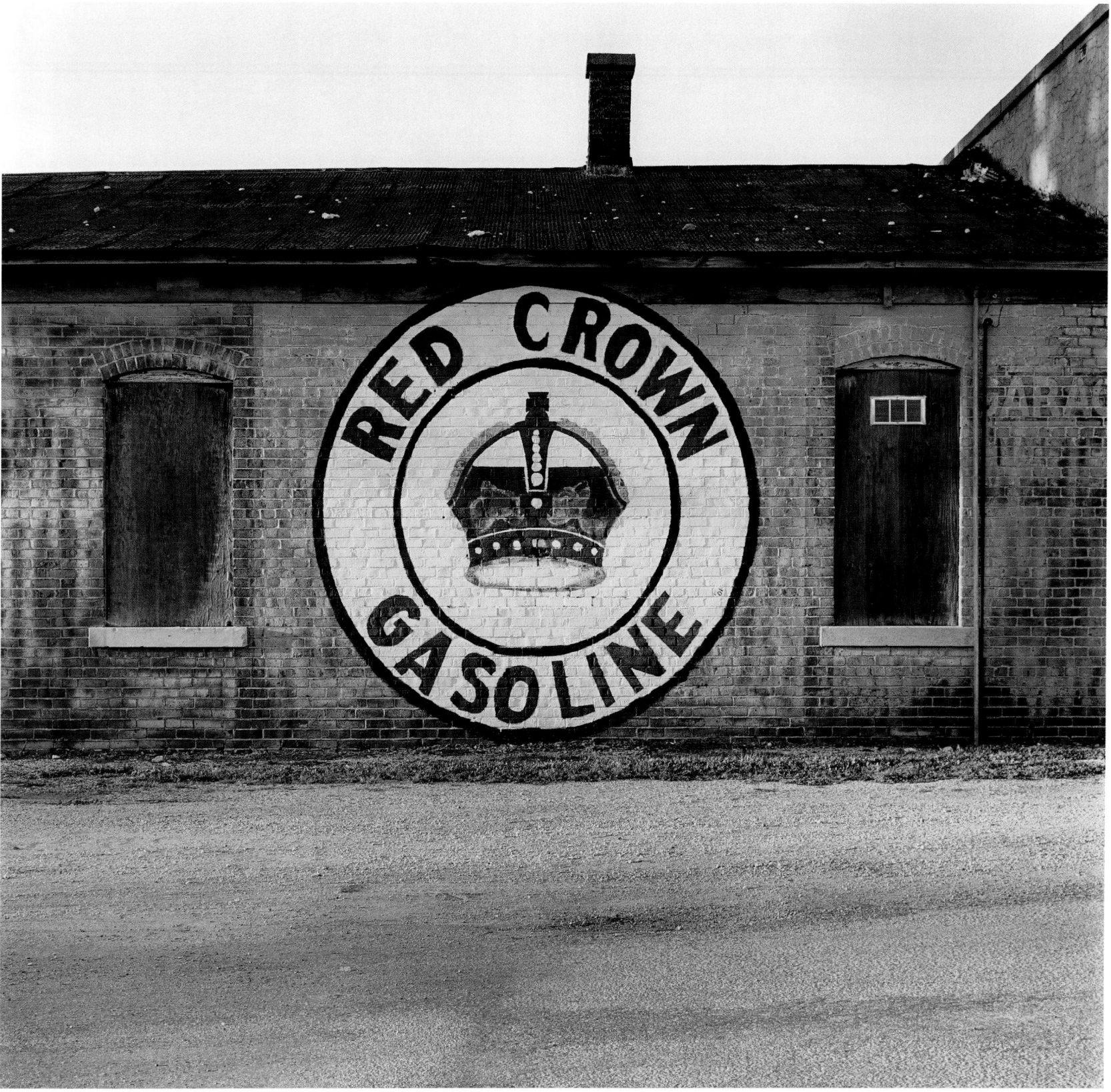

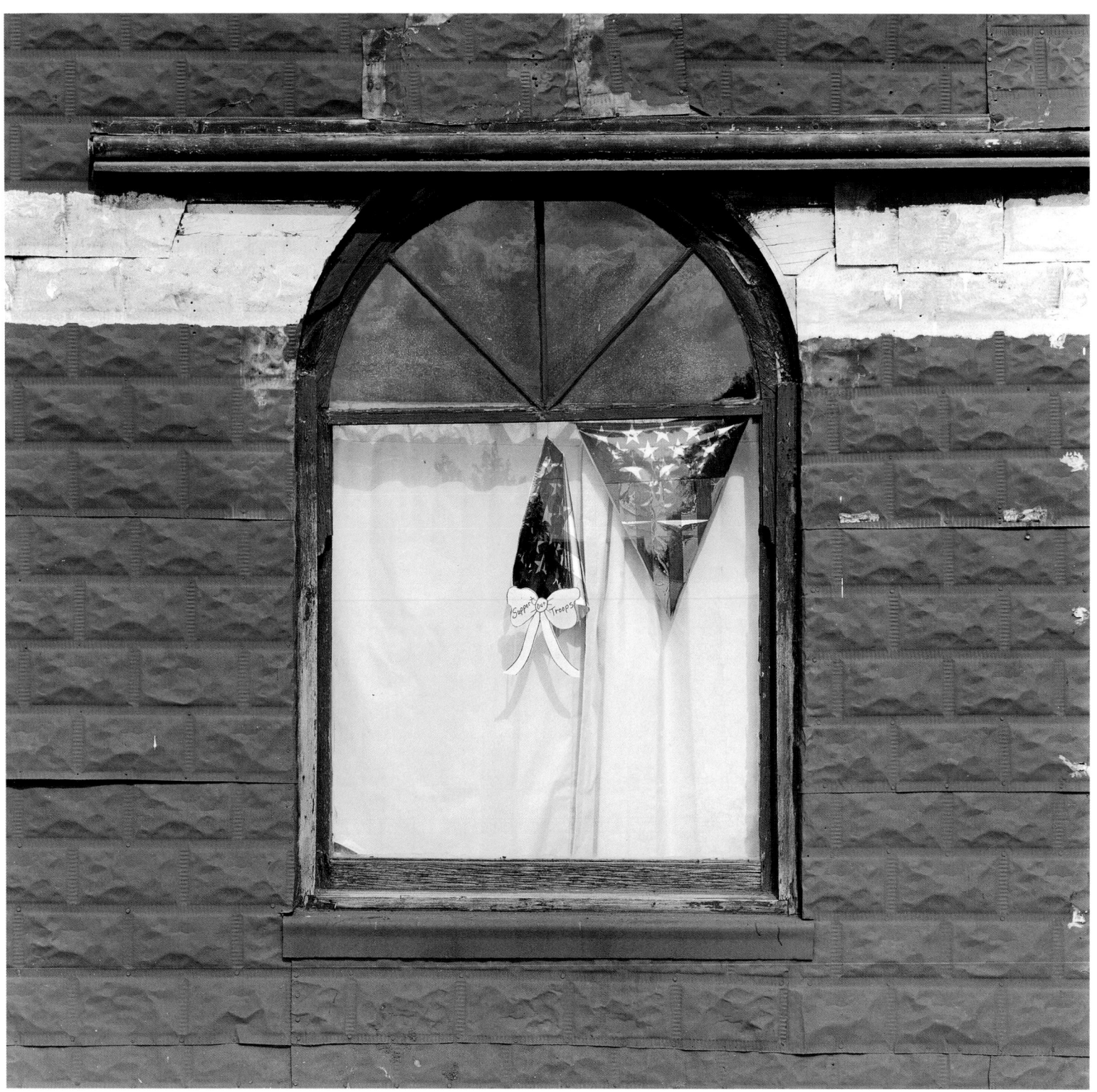

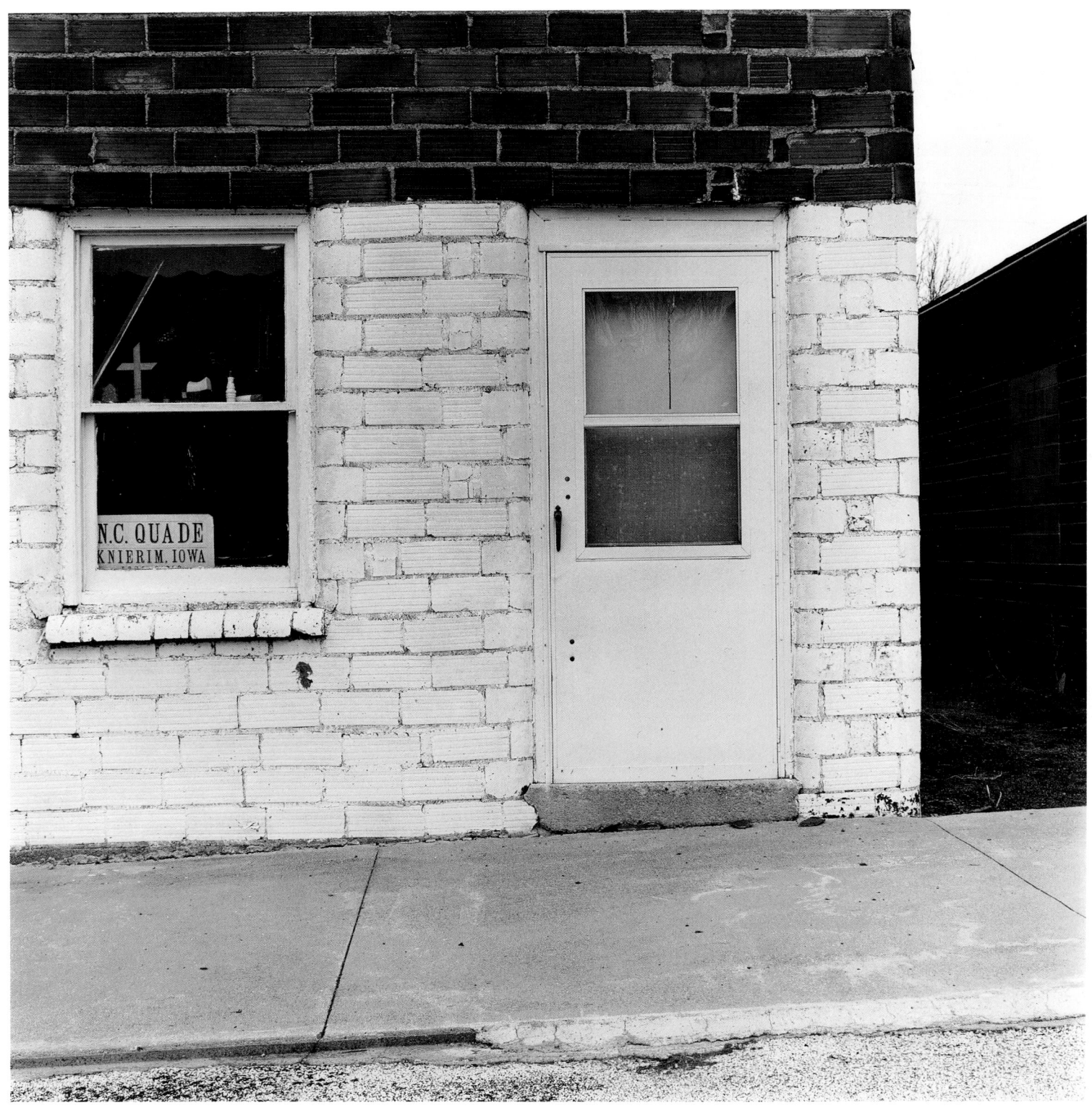

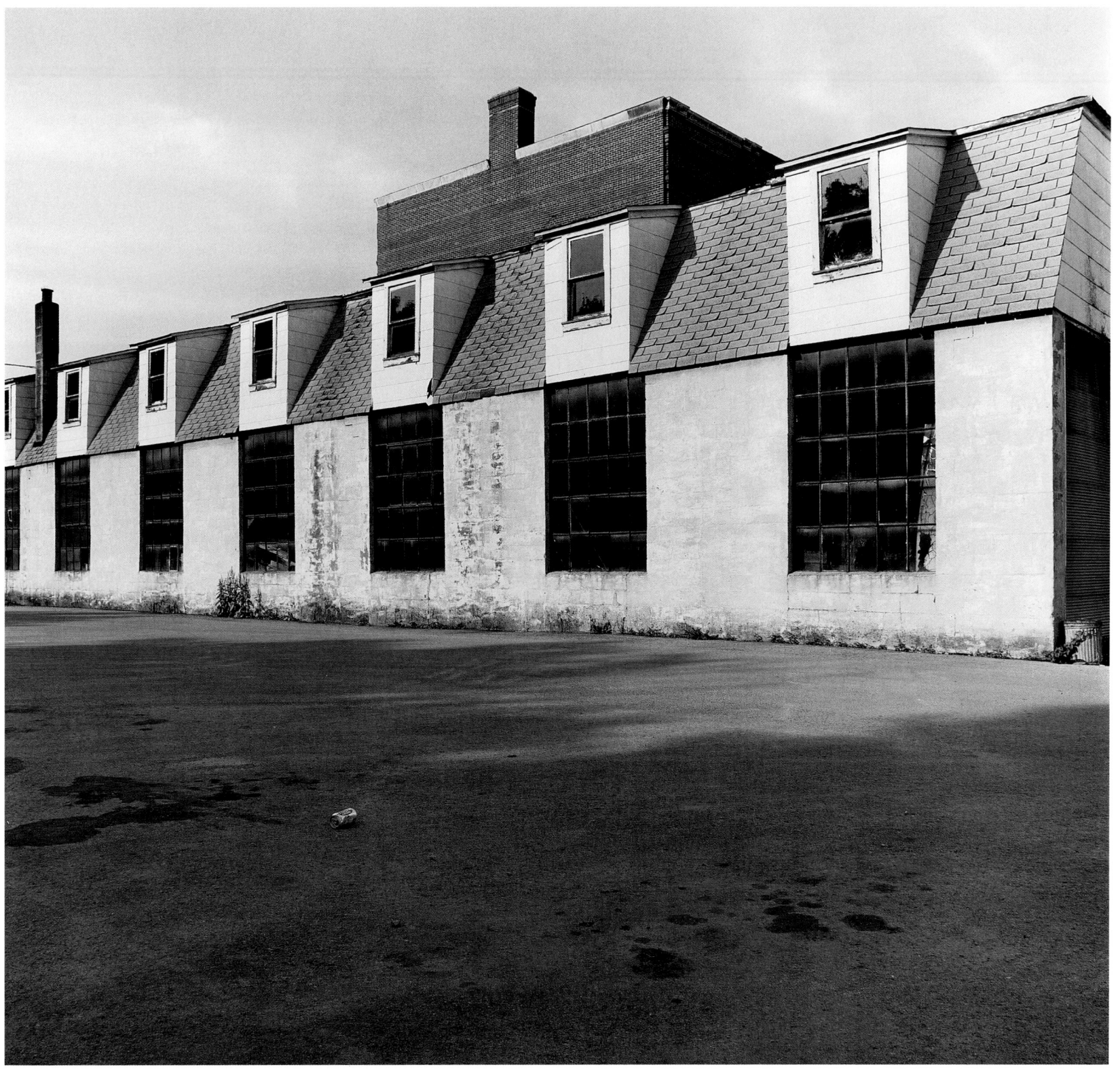

28 · Abandoned Car Barn, Punxsutawney, Pennsylvania (2004)

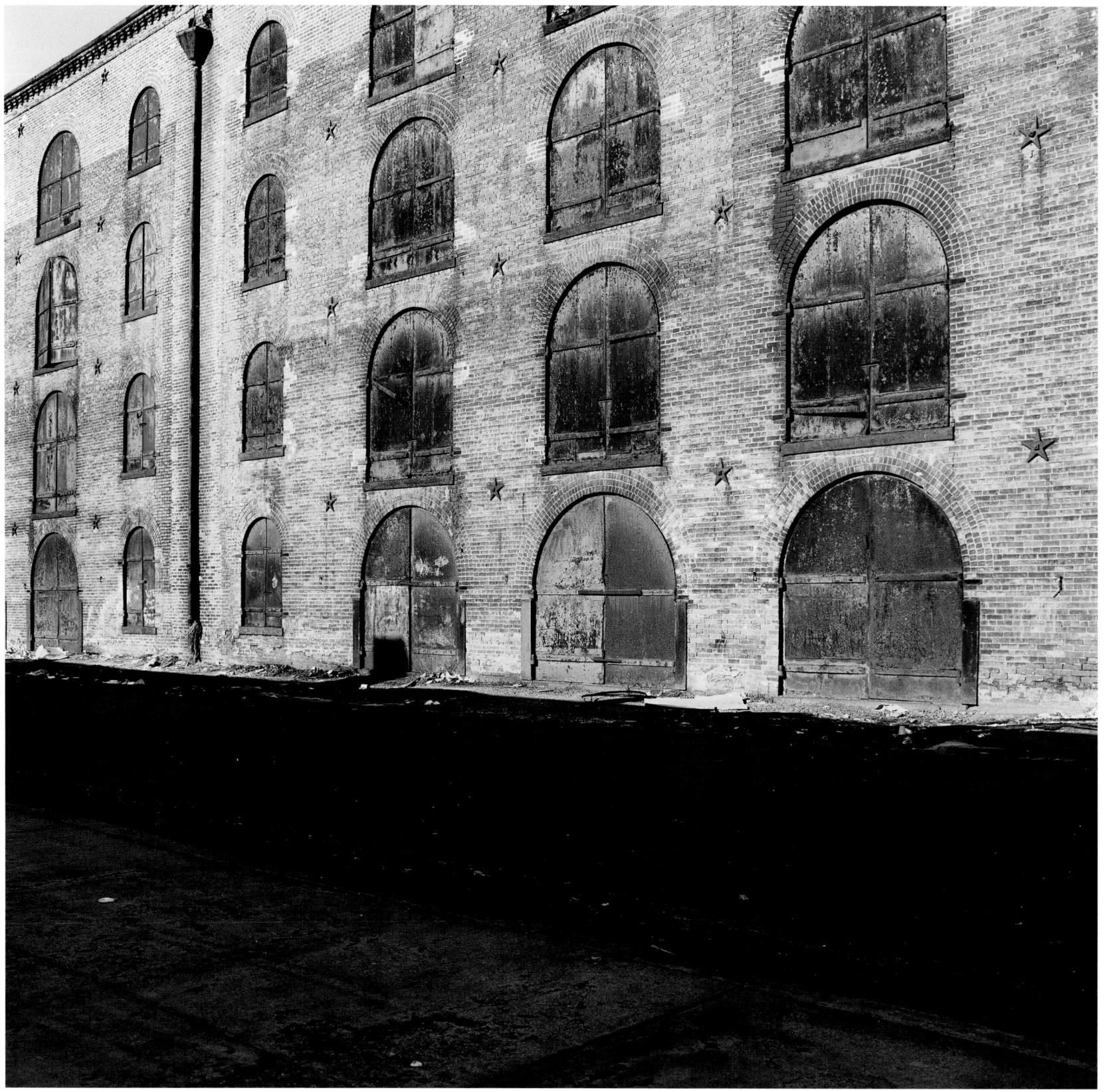

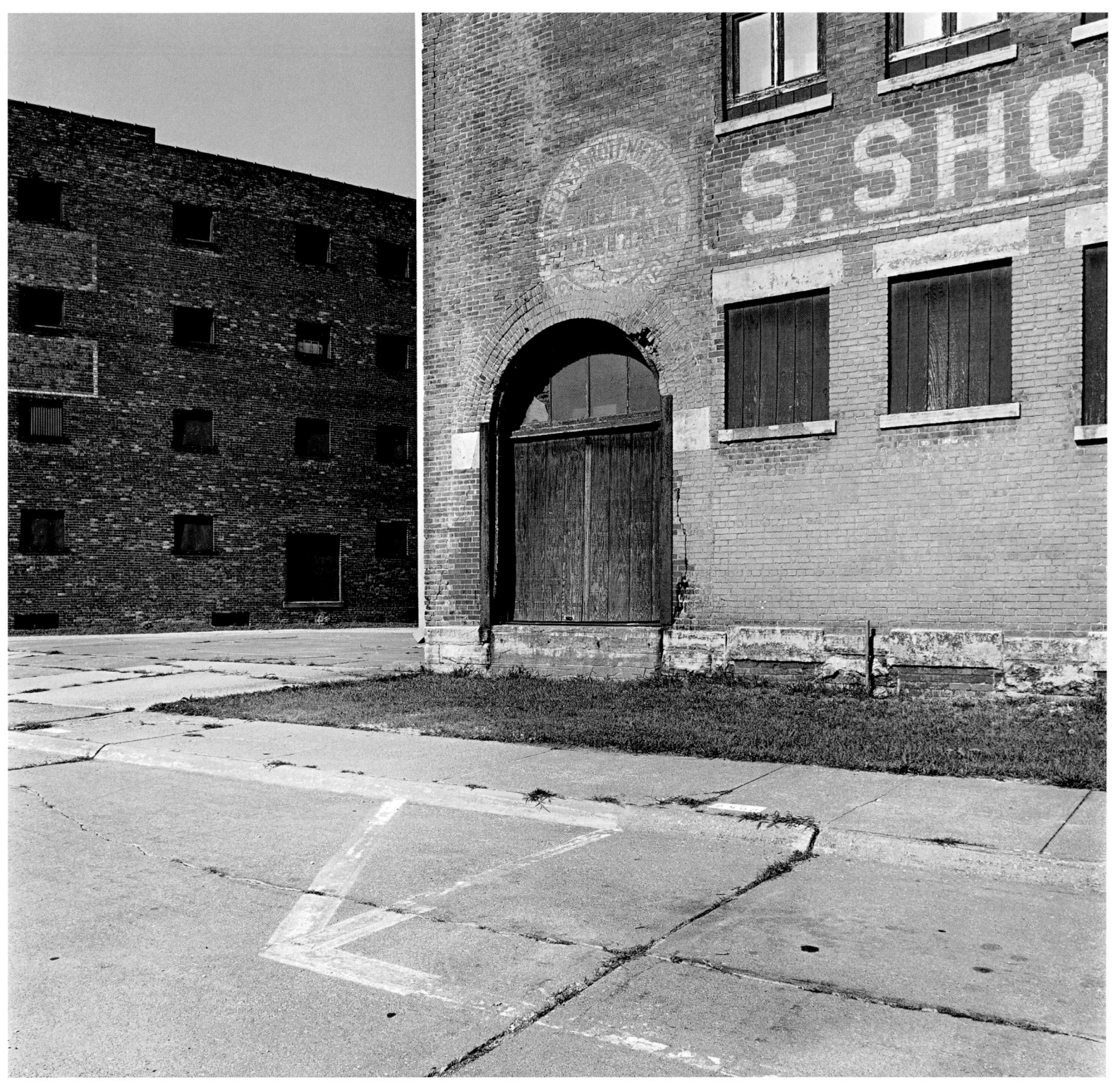

29 · Warehouse, Brooklyn, New York (1973) / 30 · Factory Buildings, Clinton, Iowa (2003)

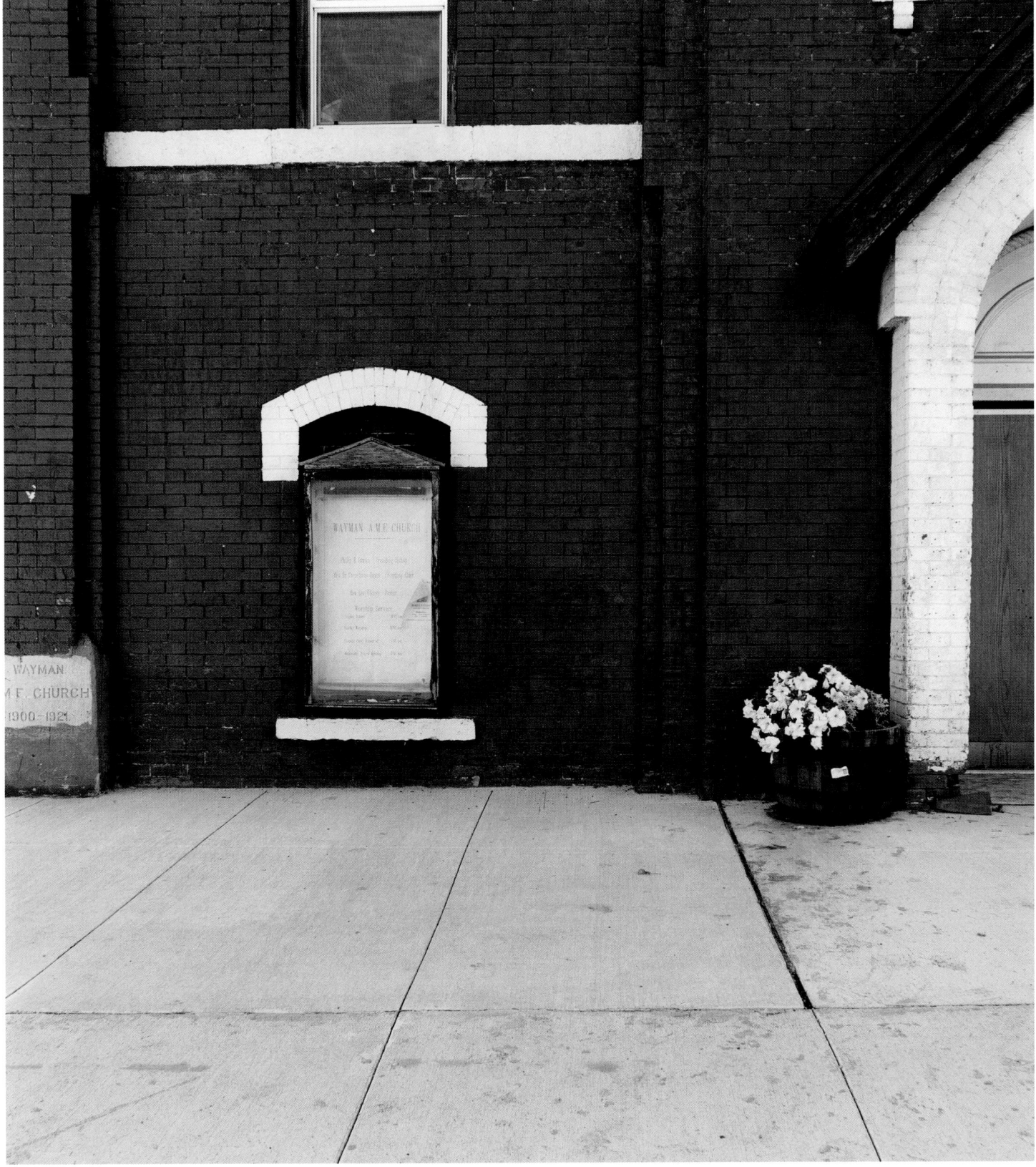

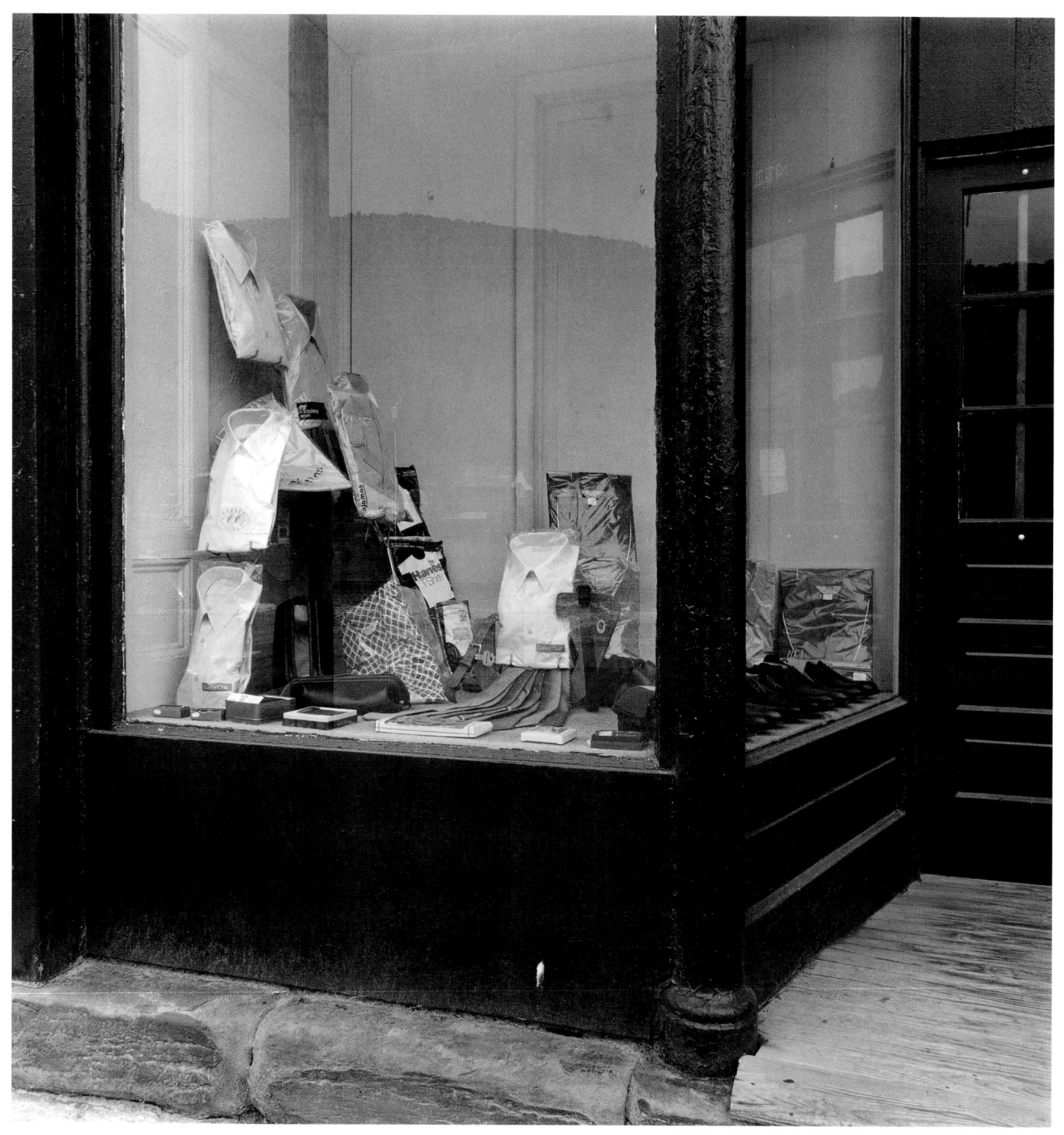

32 · Sol Mark's Clothing Store, Renovo, Pennsylvania (2004) / 33 · Holden Drugs, Chicago, Illinois (2000)

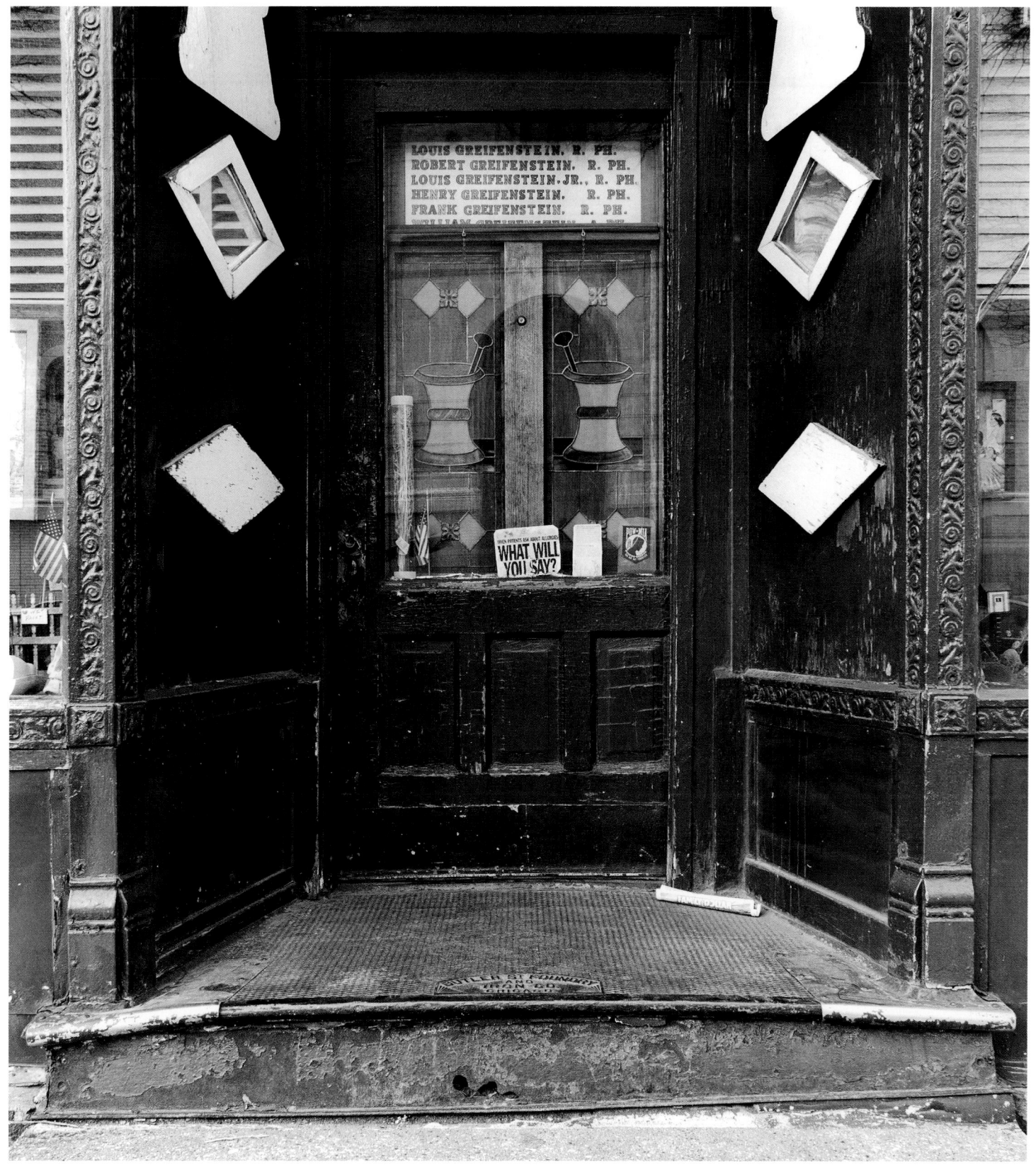

LOUIS GREIFENSTEIN. R. PH.
ROBERT GREIFENSTEIN. R. PH.
LOUIS GREIFENSTEIN, JR., R. PH.
HENRY GREIFENSTEIN. R. PH.
FRANK GREIFENSTEIN. R. PH.

WHAT WILL YOU SAY?

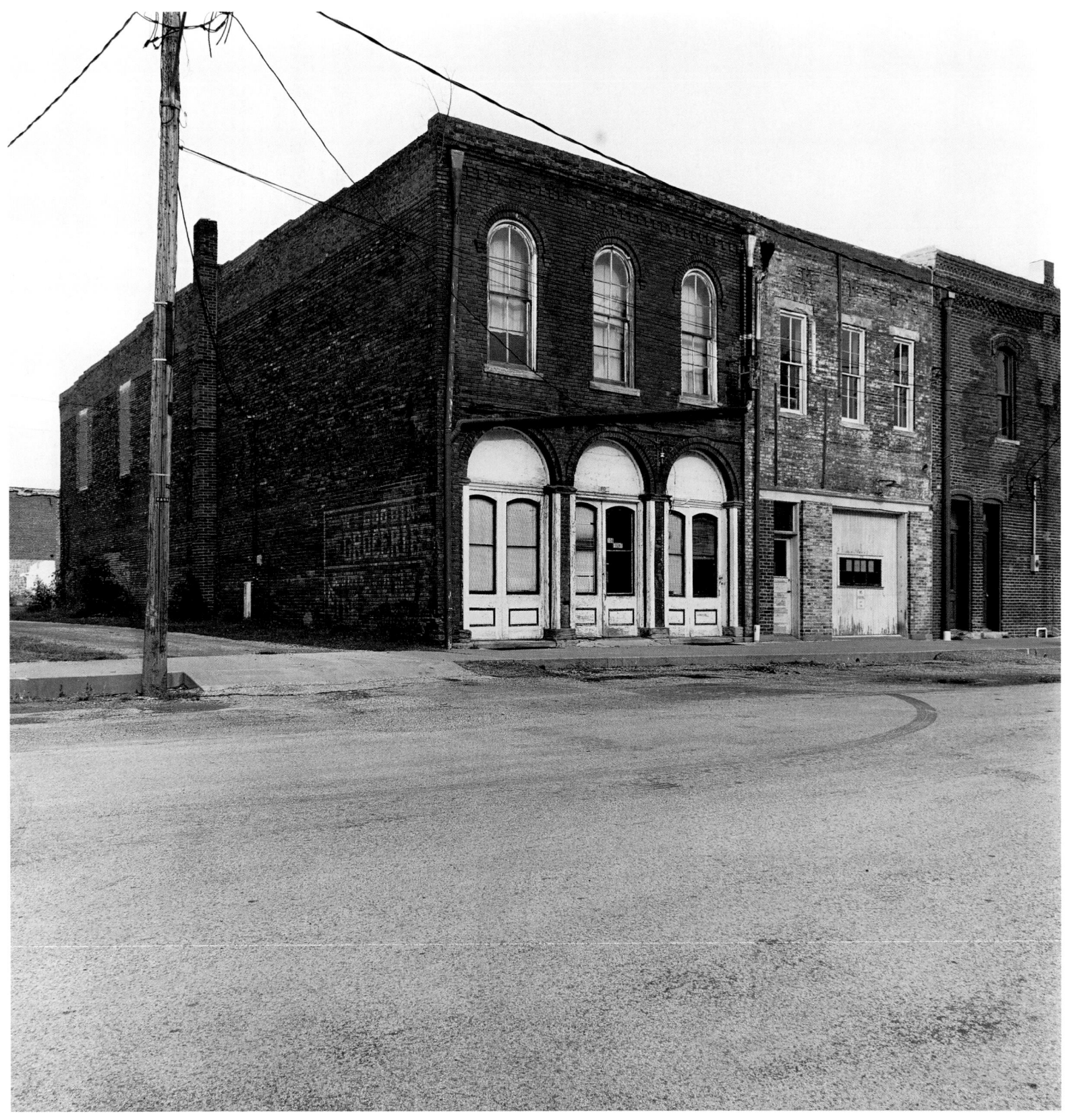

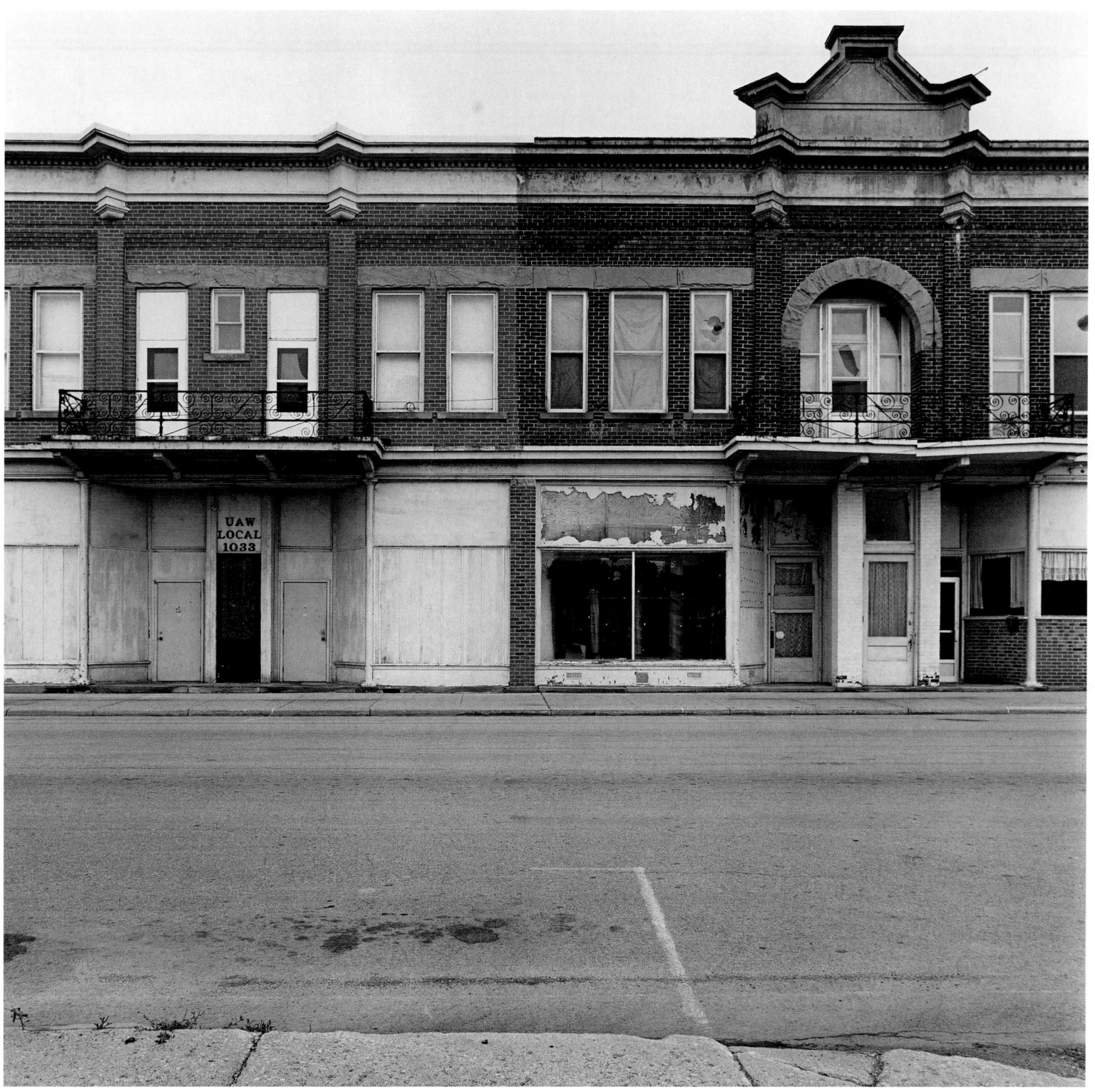

34 · Farmington, Iowa (2004)   /   35 · Forest, Ohio (2003)

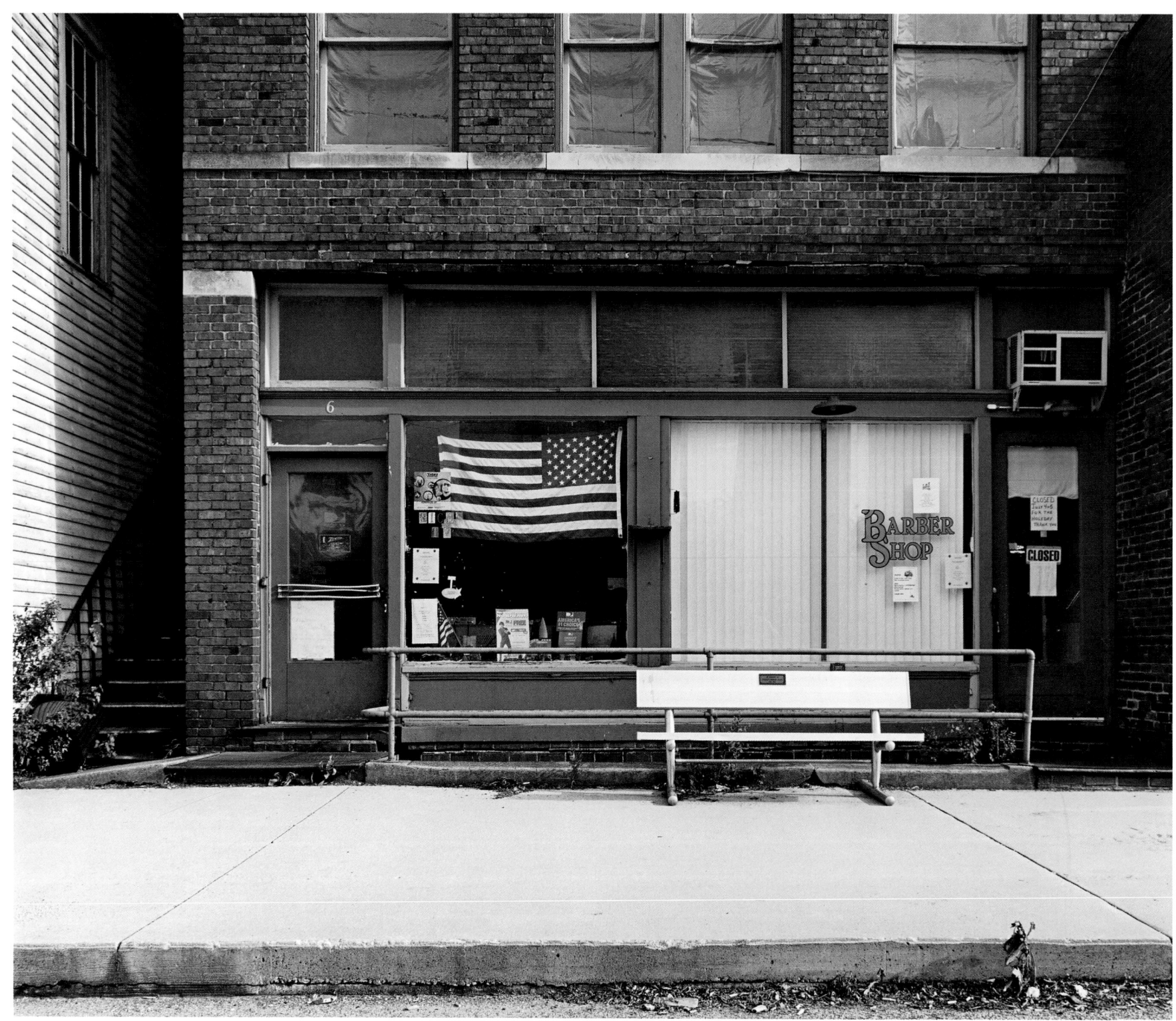

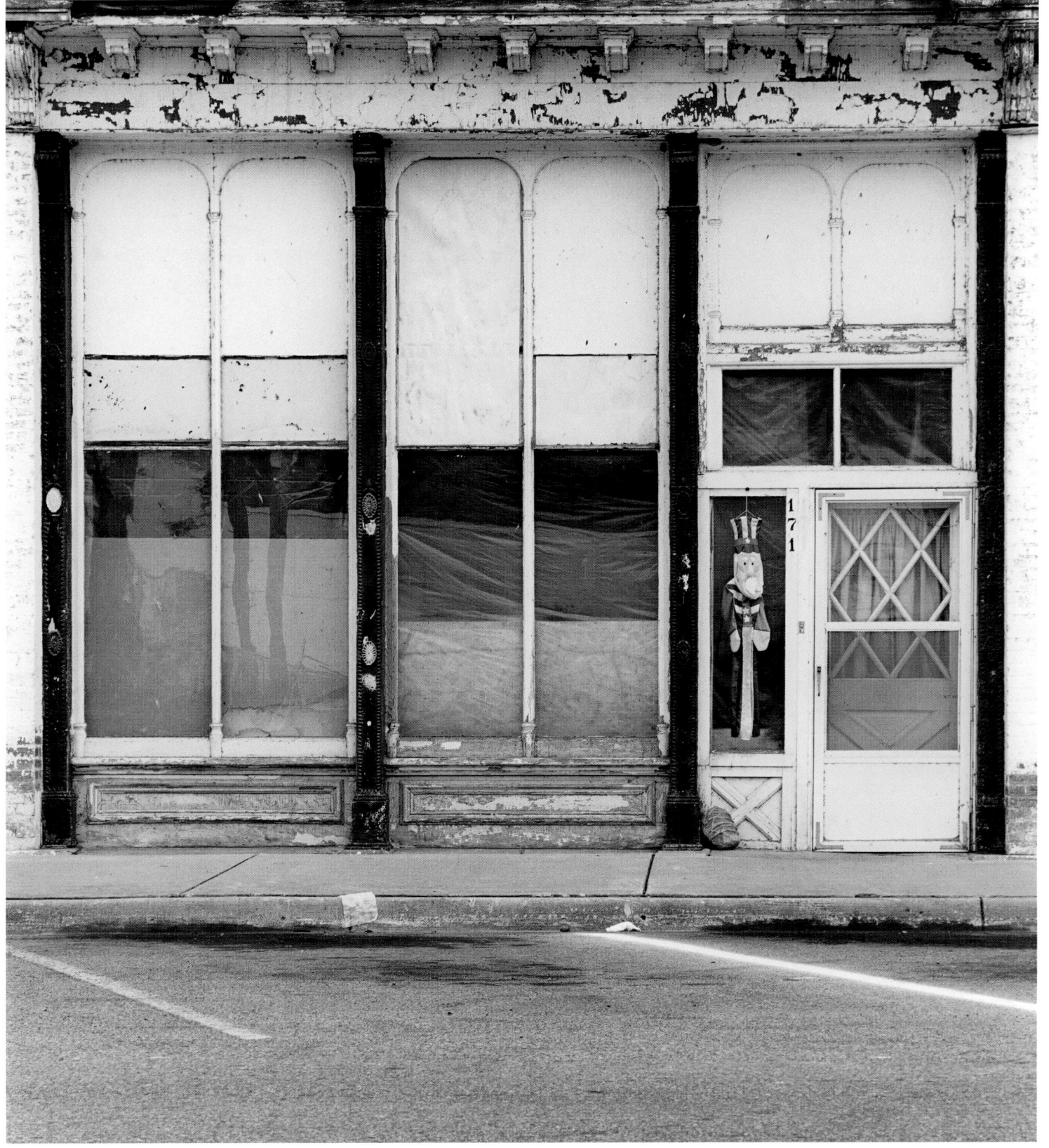

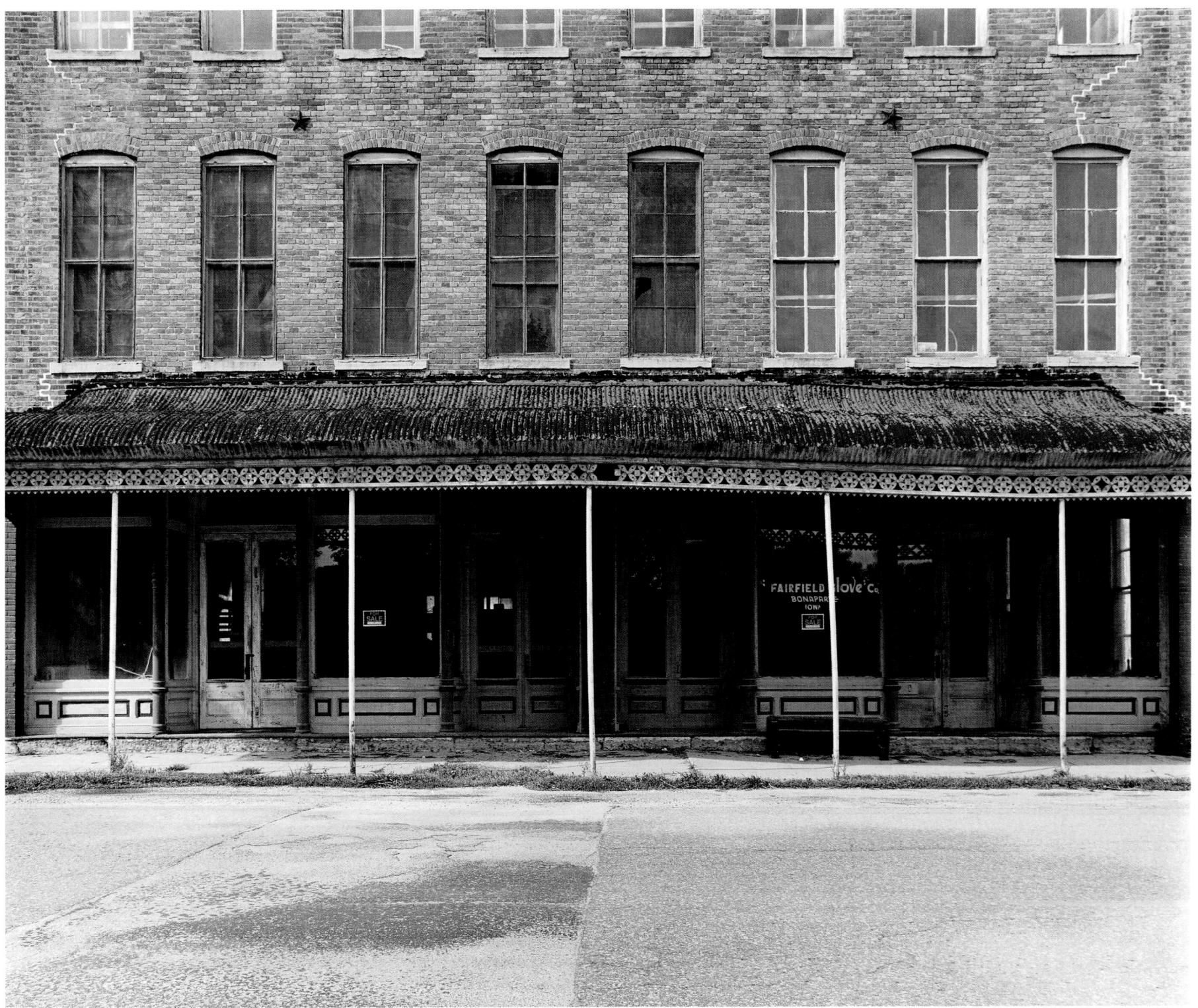

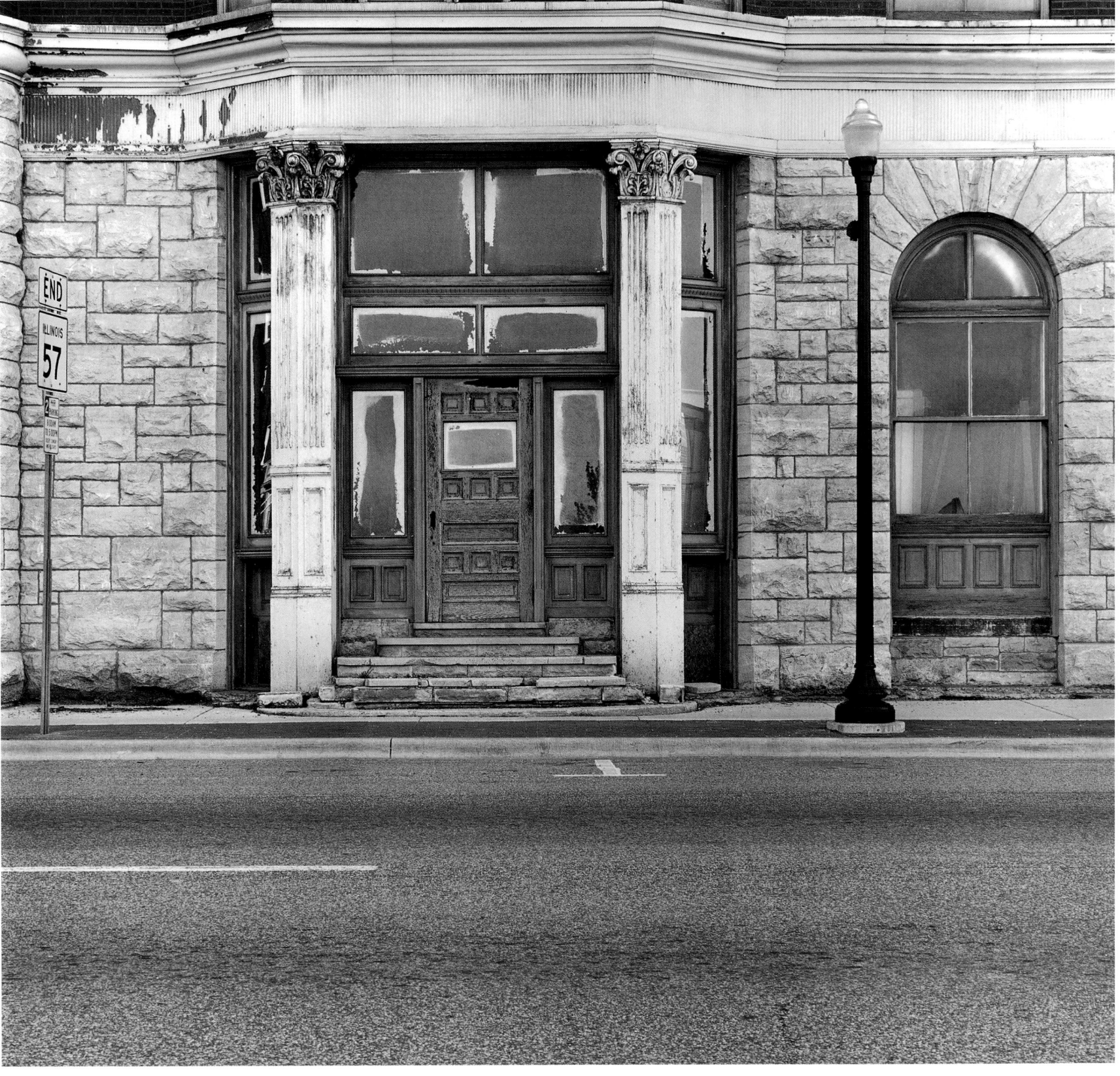

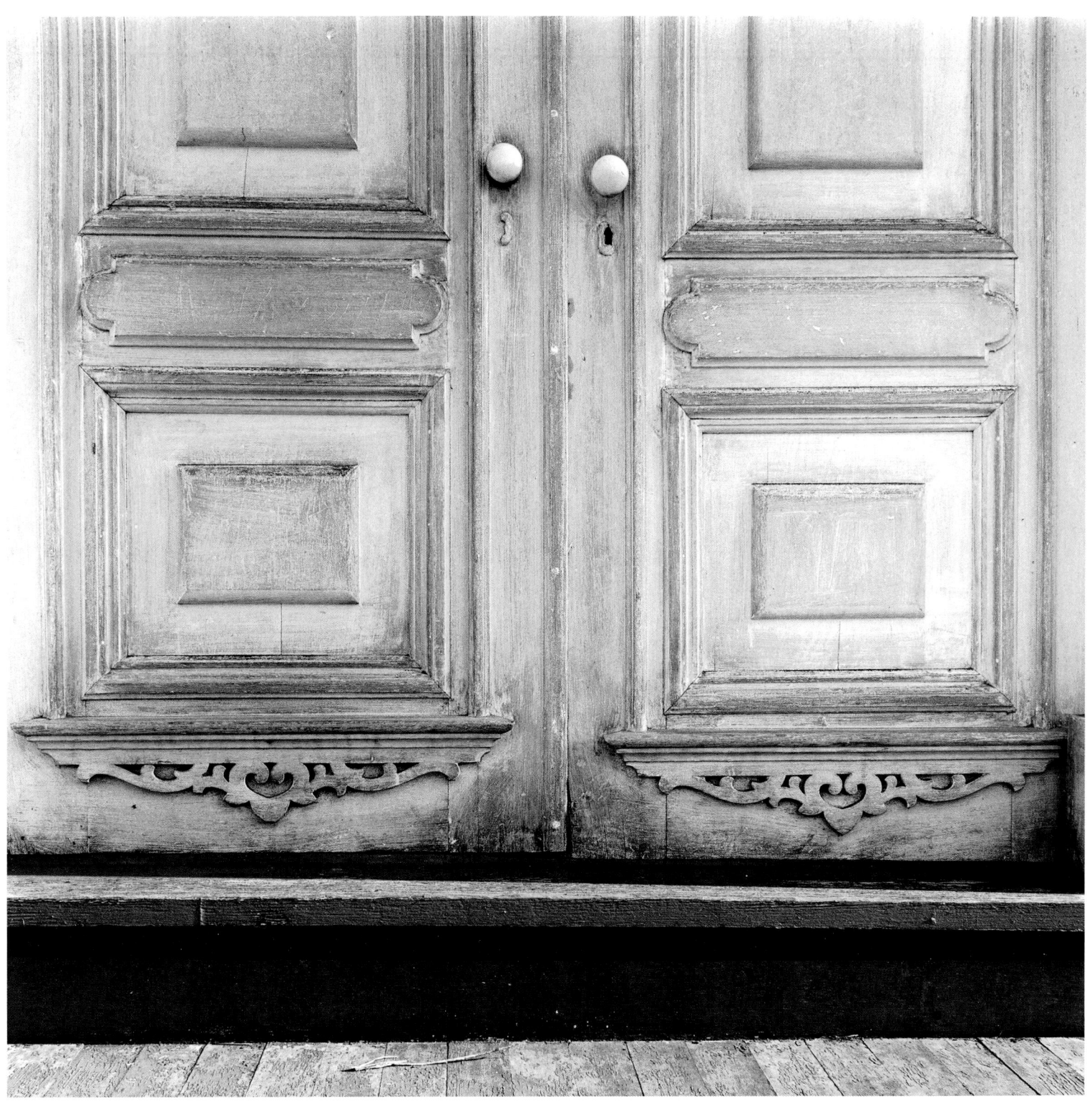

40 · Church Doorway, Auriesville, New York (1964)

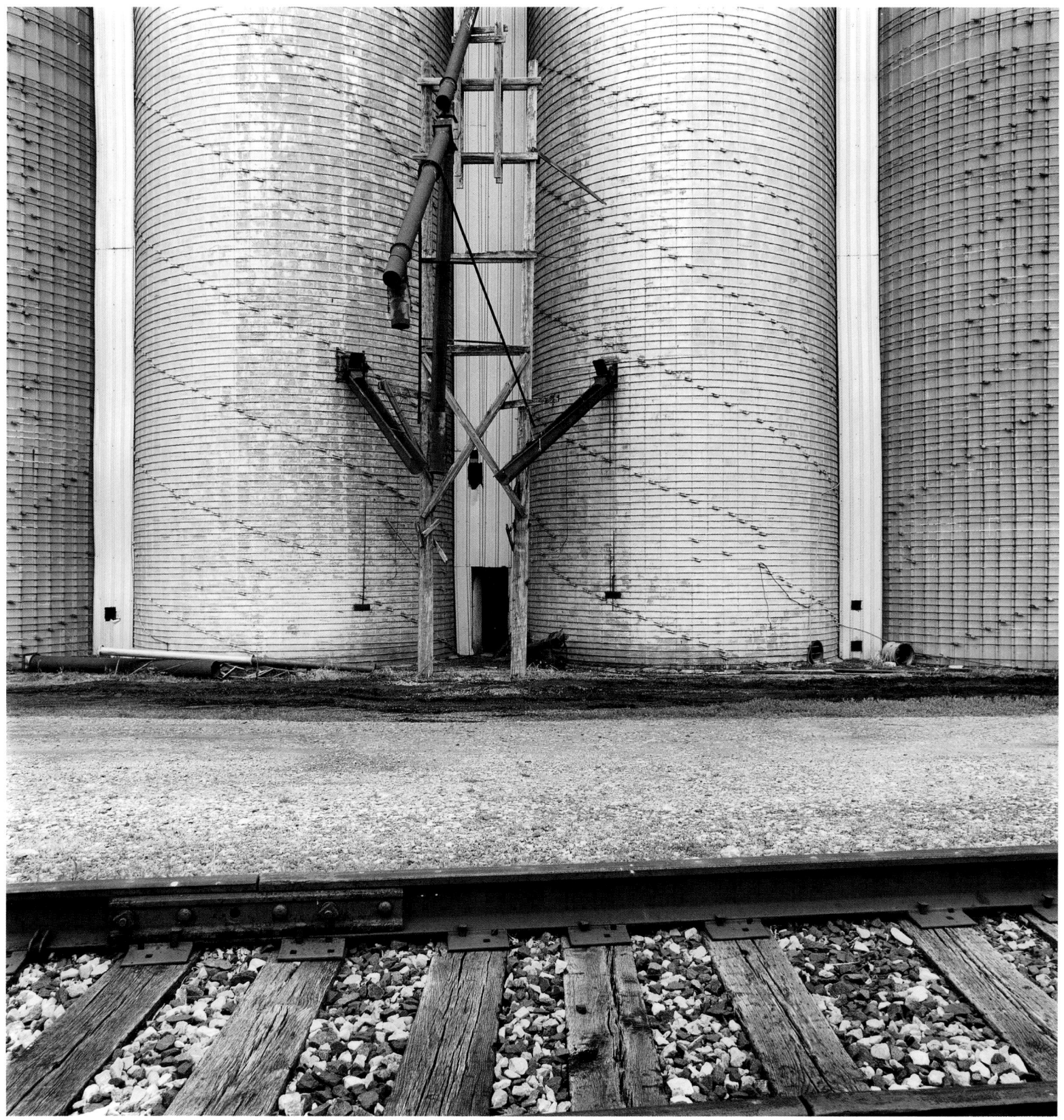

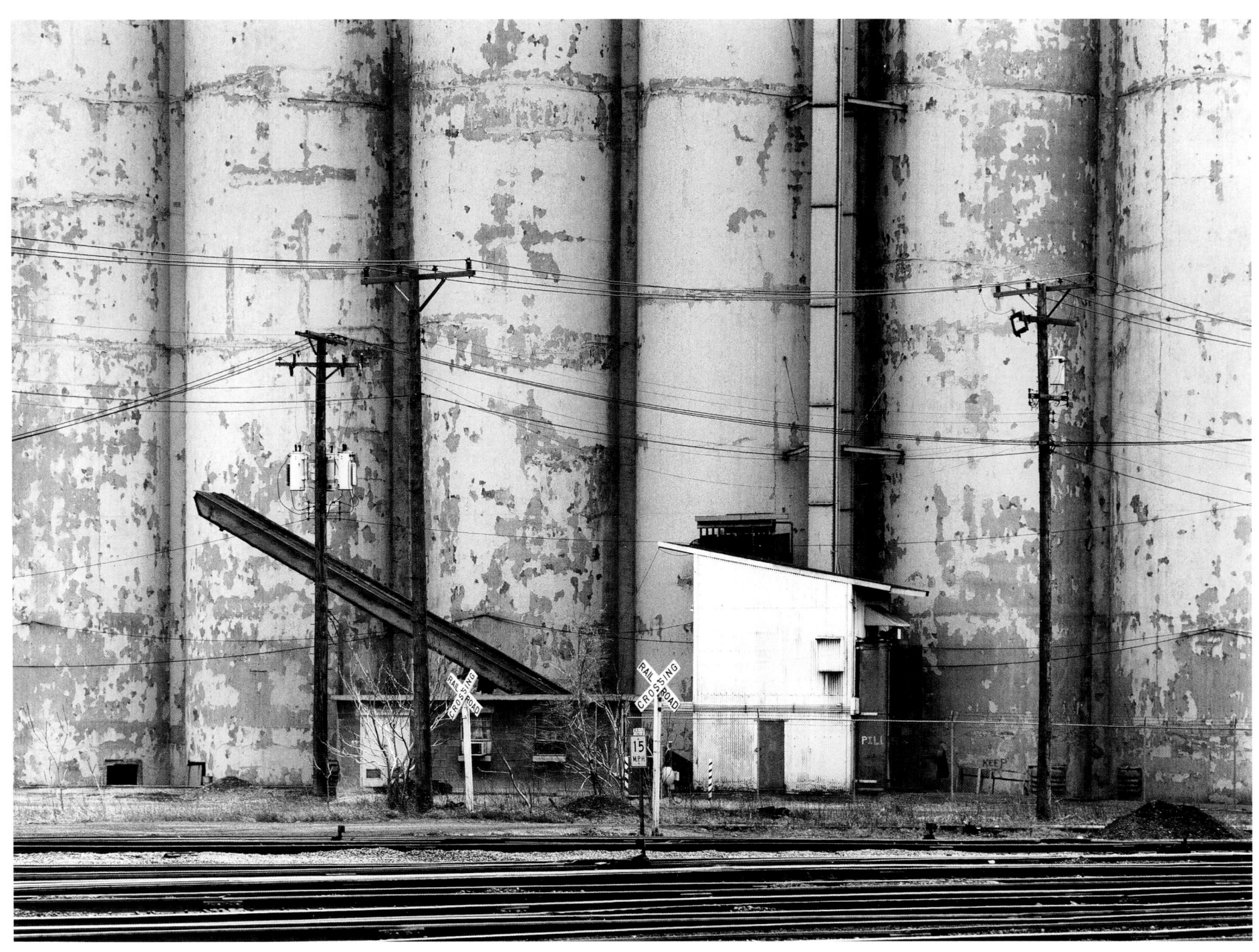

42 · Grain Elevator, Chicago, Illinois (1979)

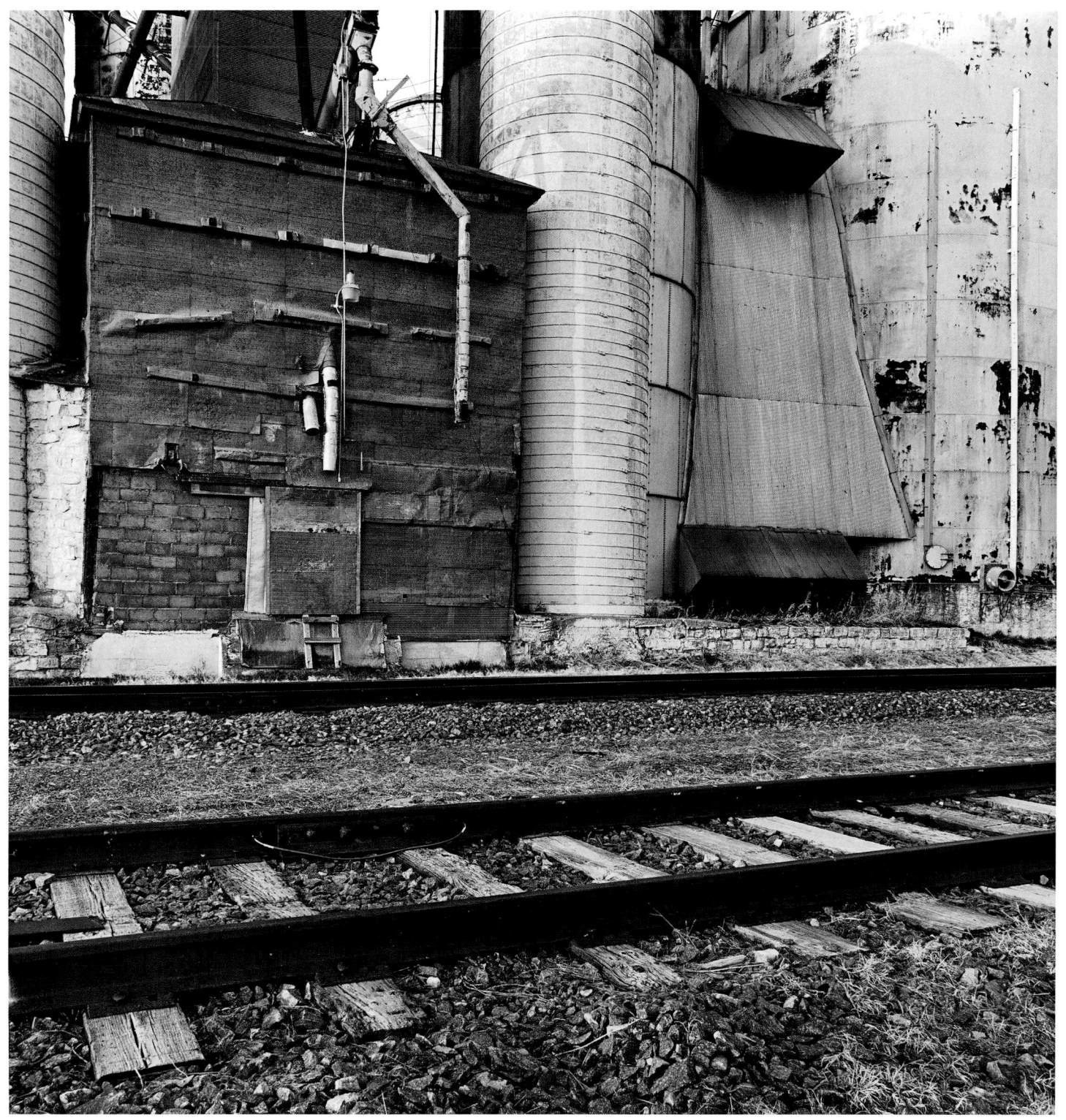

43 · Grain Elevator, Wilson, Kansas (2004)

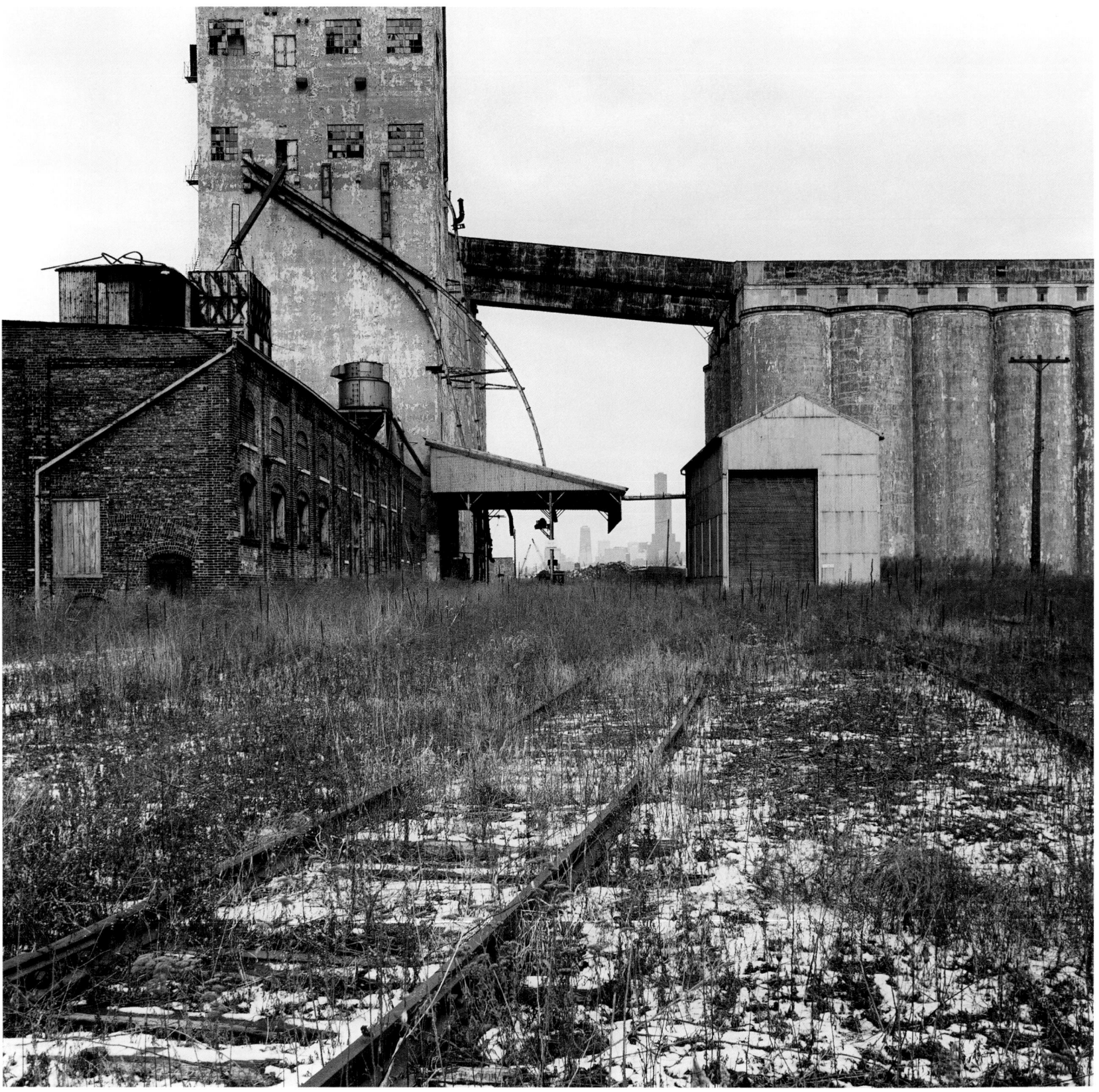

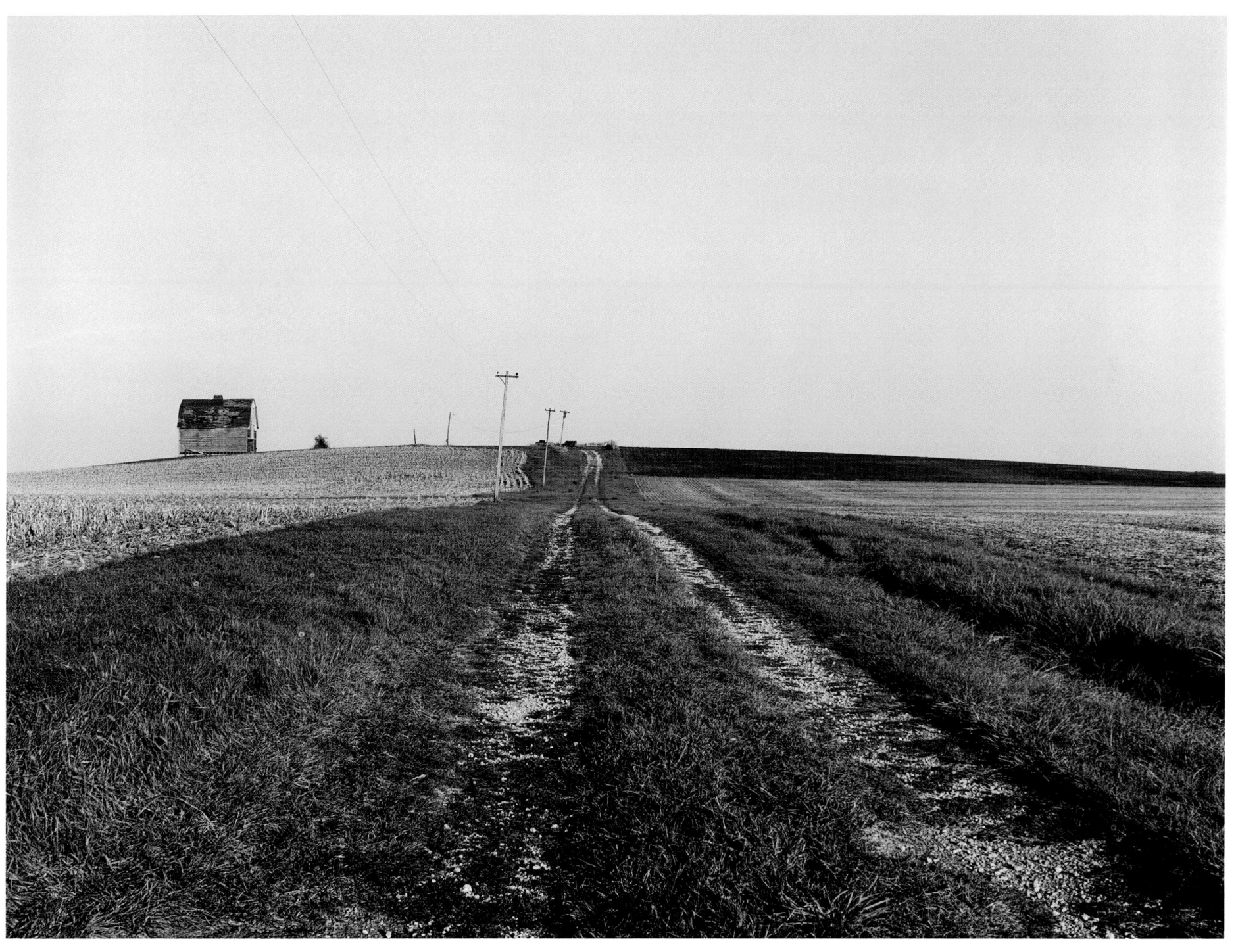

44 · Abandoned Grain Elevator, Chicago, Illinois (1983) / 45 · Owego Township, Livingston County, Illinois (2003)

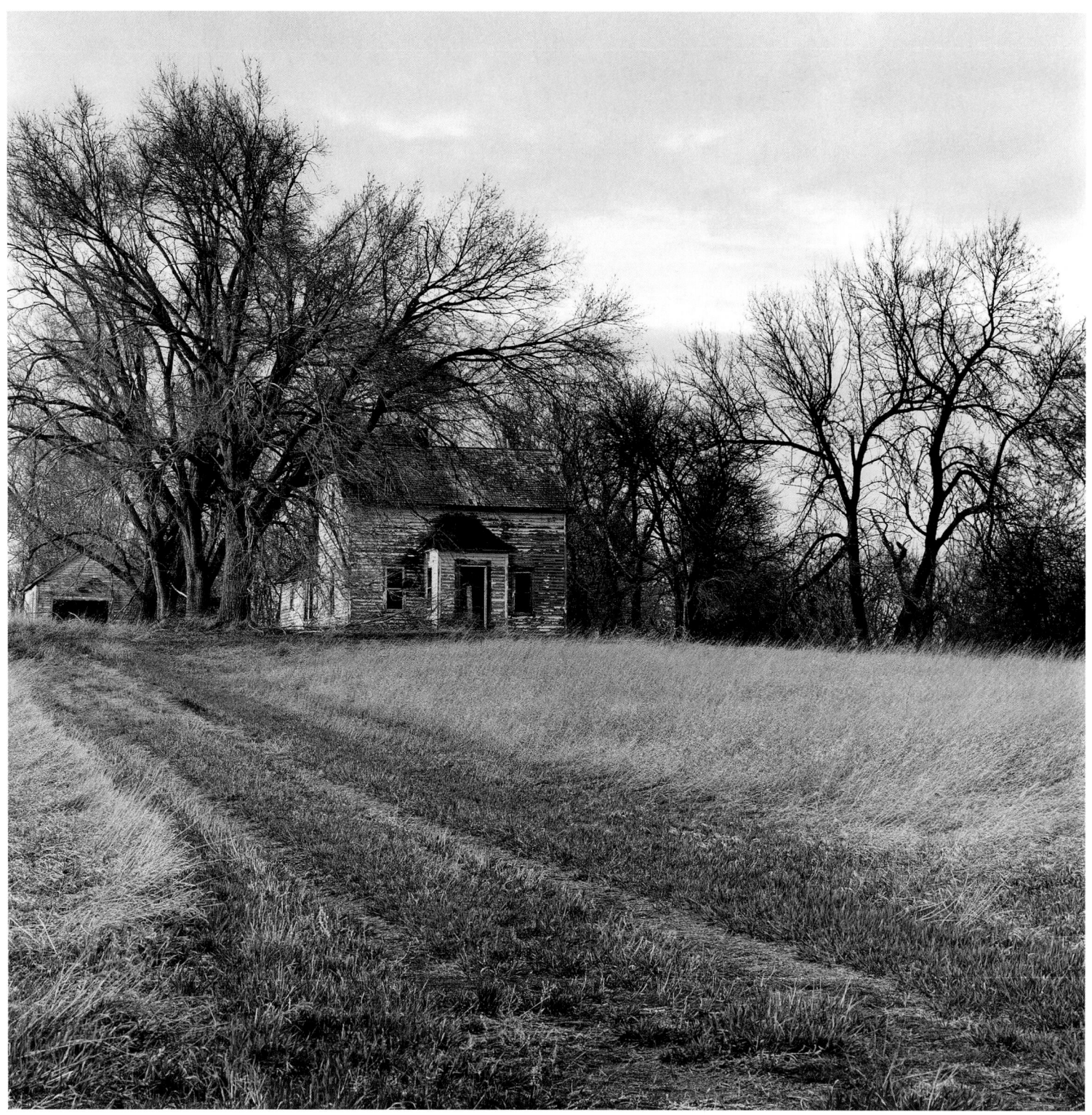

46 · Cedar County, Nebraska (2004) / 47 · East of Dwight, Kansas (1991)

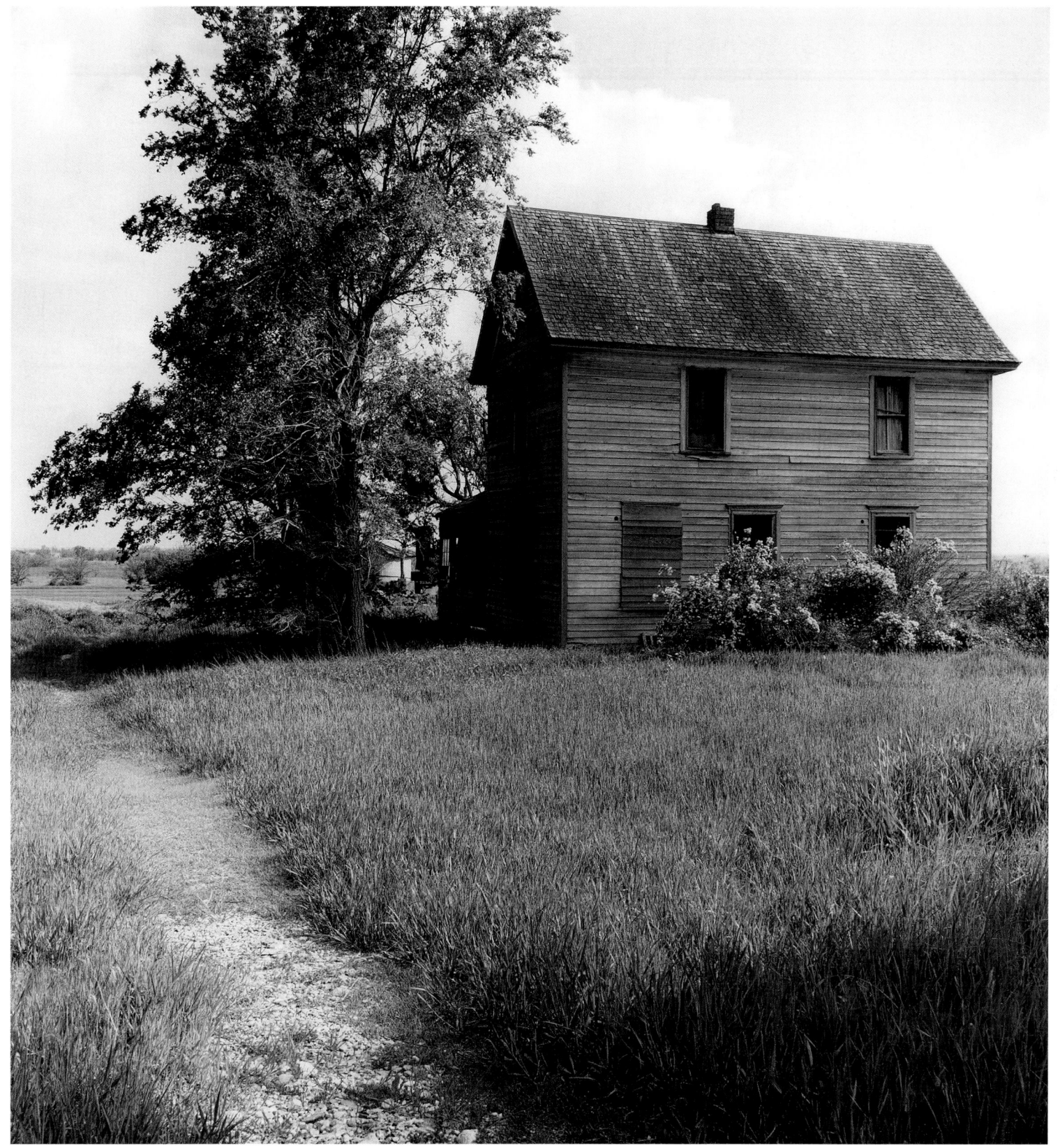

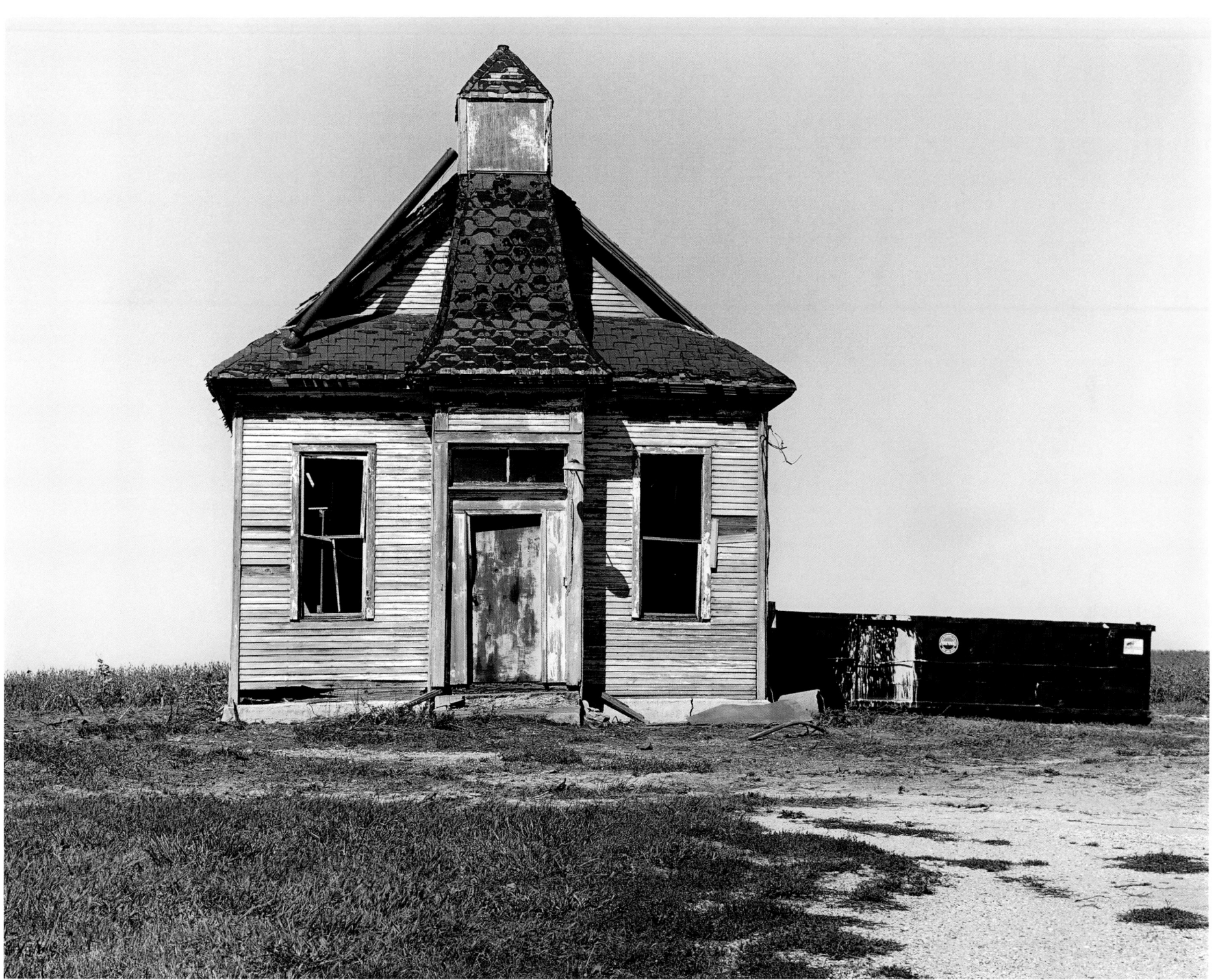

48 · Abandoned Schoolhouse, Peoria County, Illinois (2003)

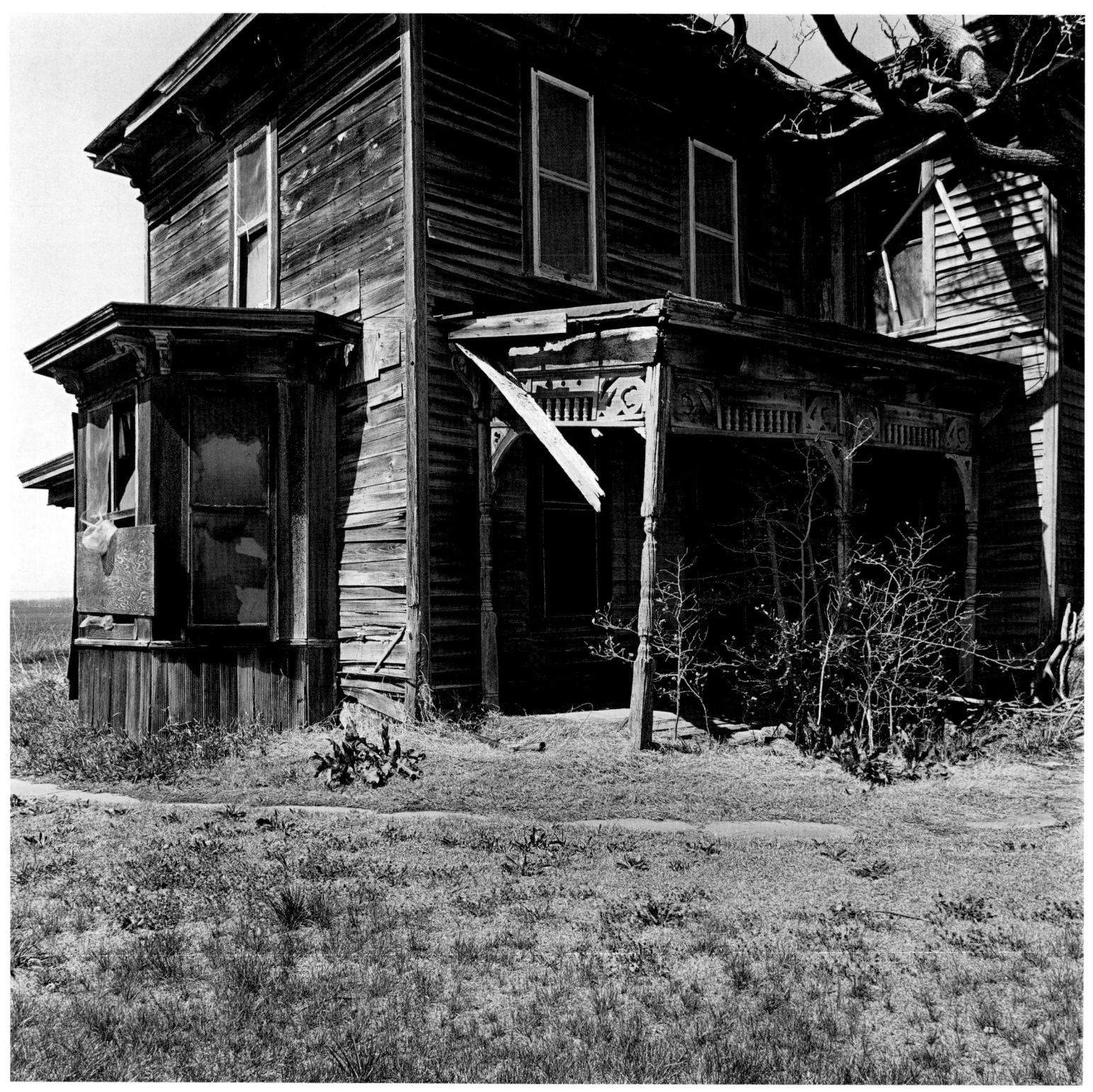

49 · Gypsum, Kansas (2004) / 50 · Deserted Farmhouse, near Bushong, Kansas (1991)

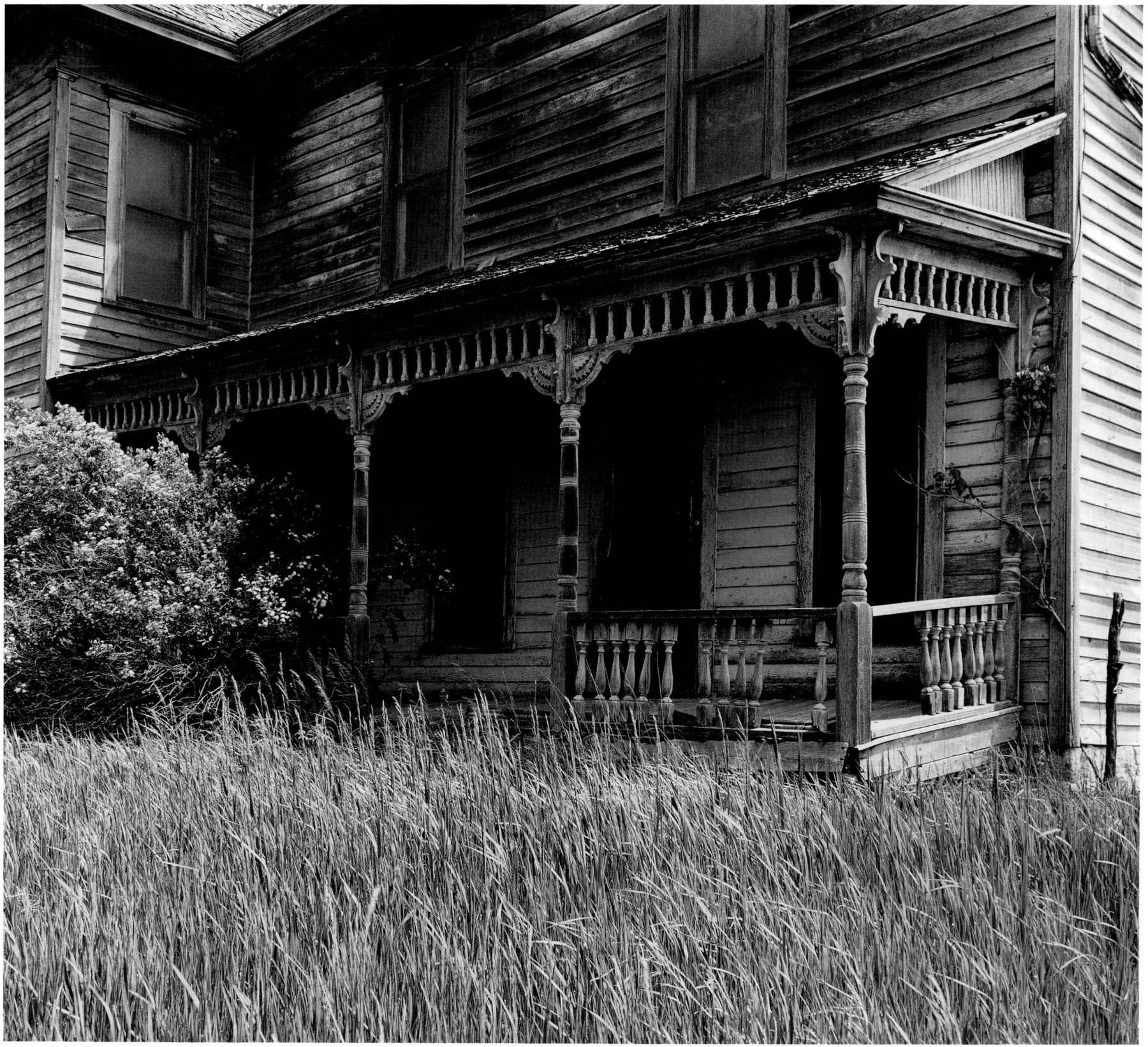

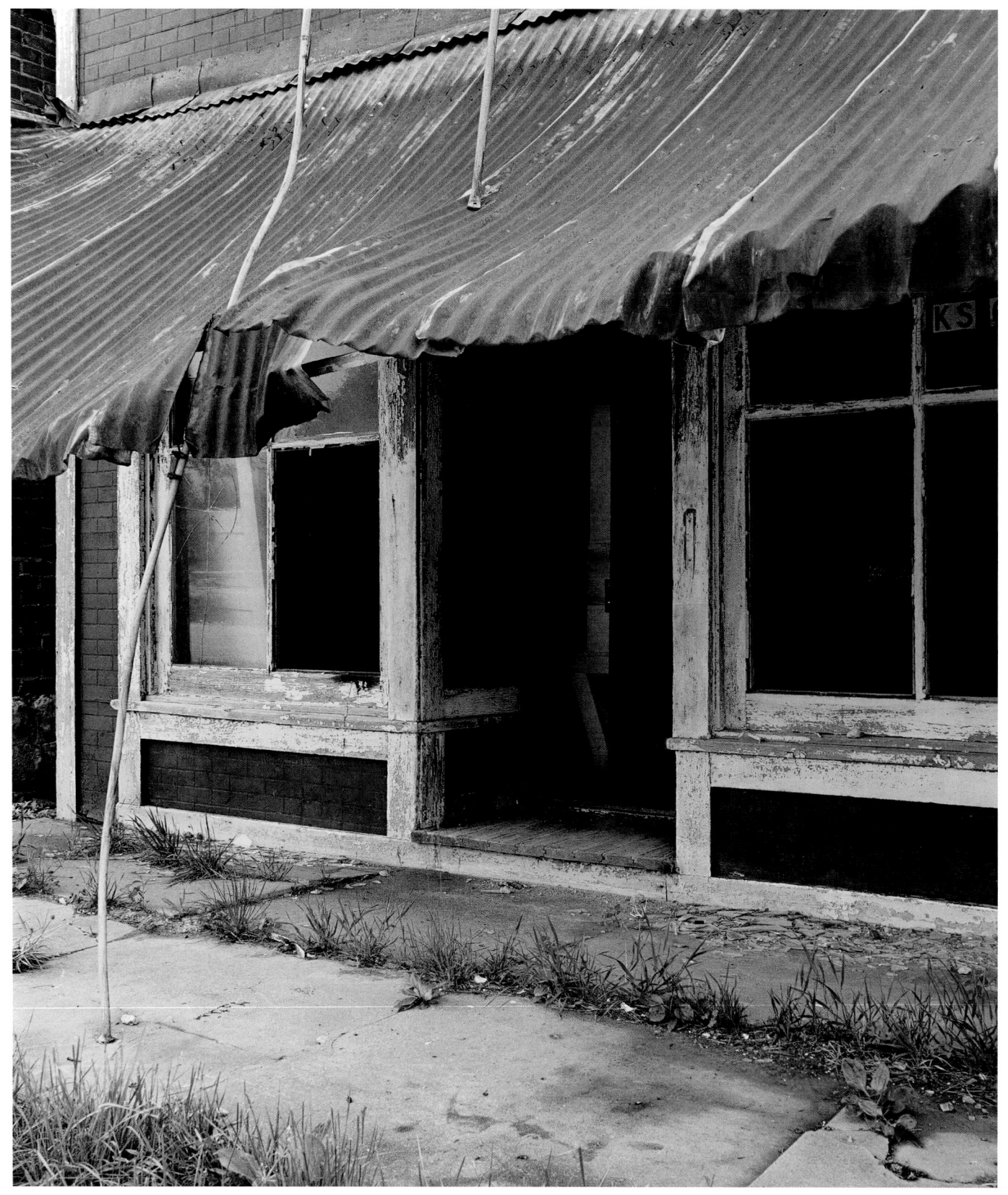

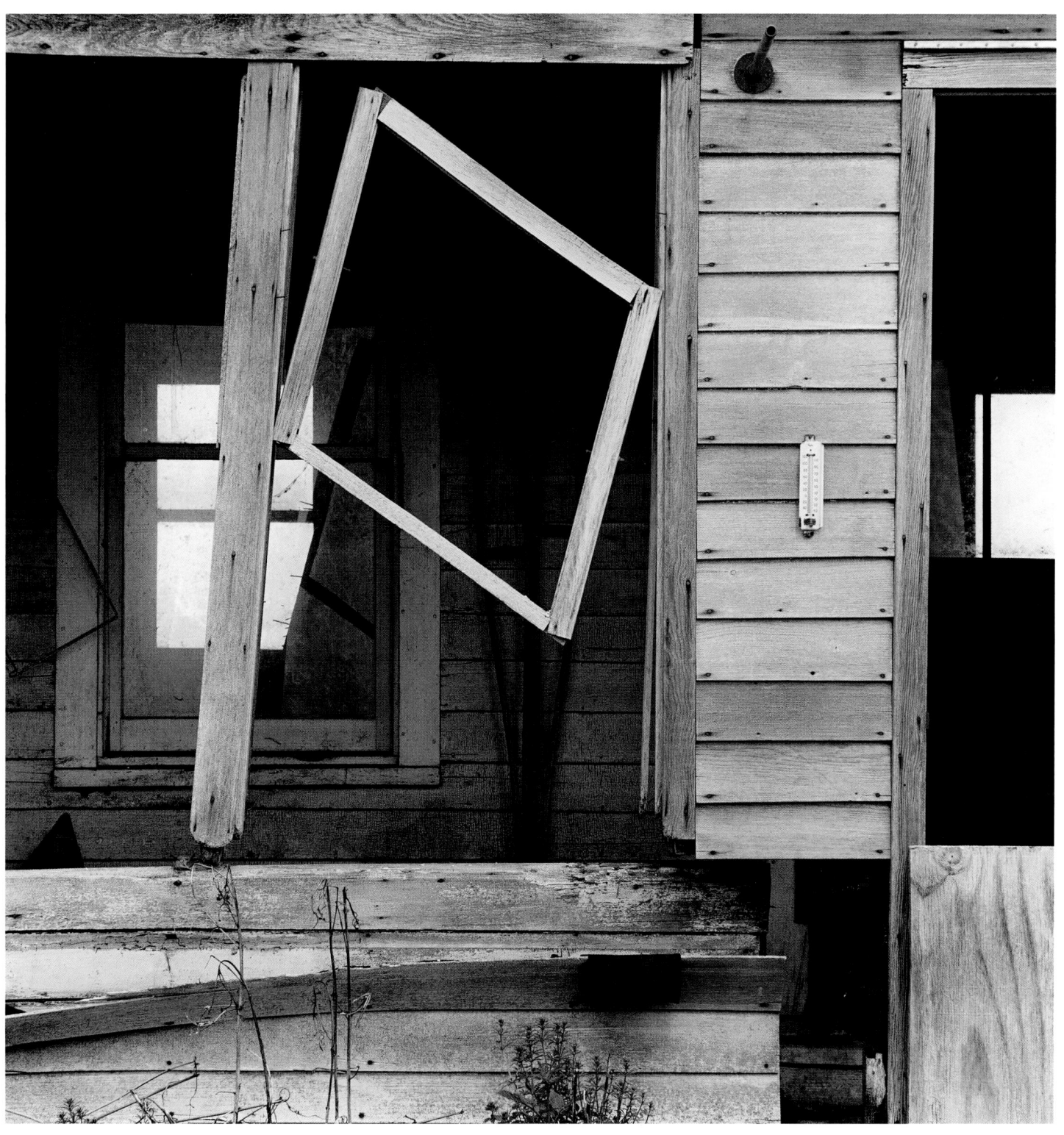

51 · Former Post Office, Bushong, Kansas (1991) / 52 · Deserted Farmhouse, West of Alta Vista, Kansas (1991)

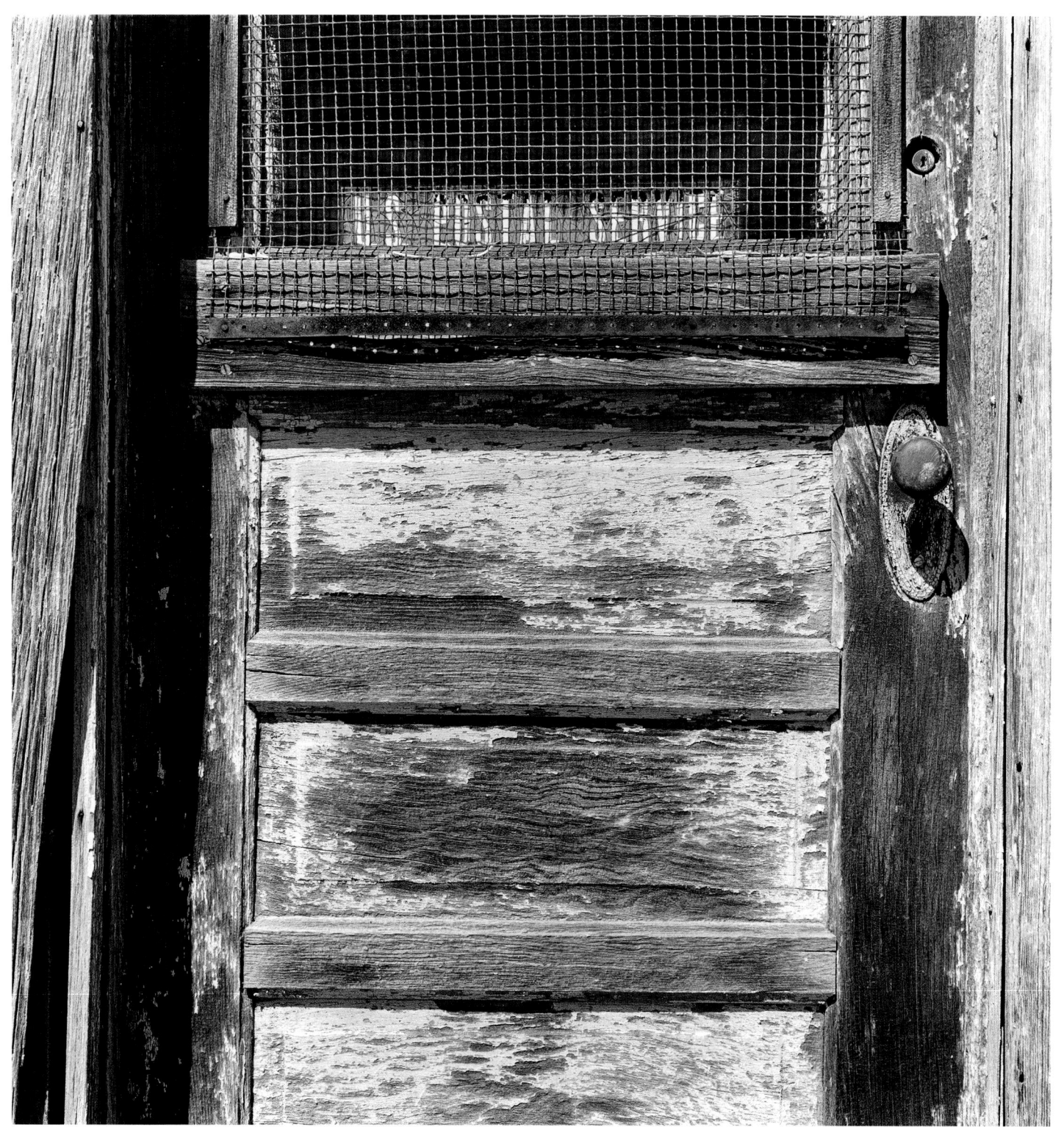

53 · Post Office Doorway, Carlton, Kansas (2004)

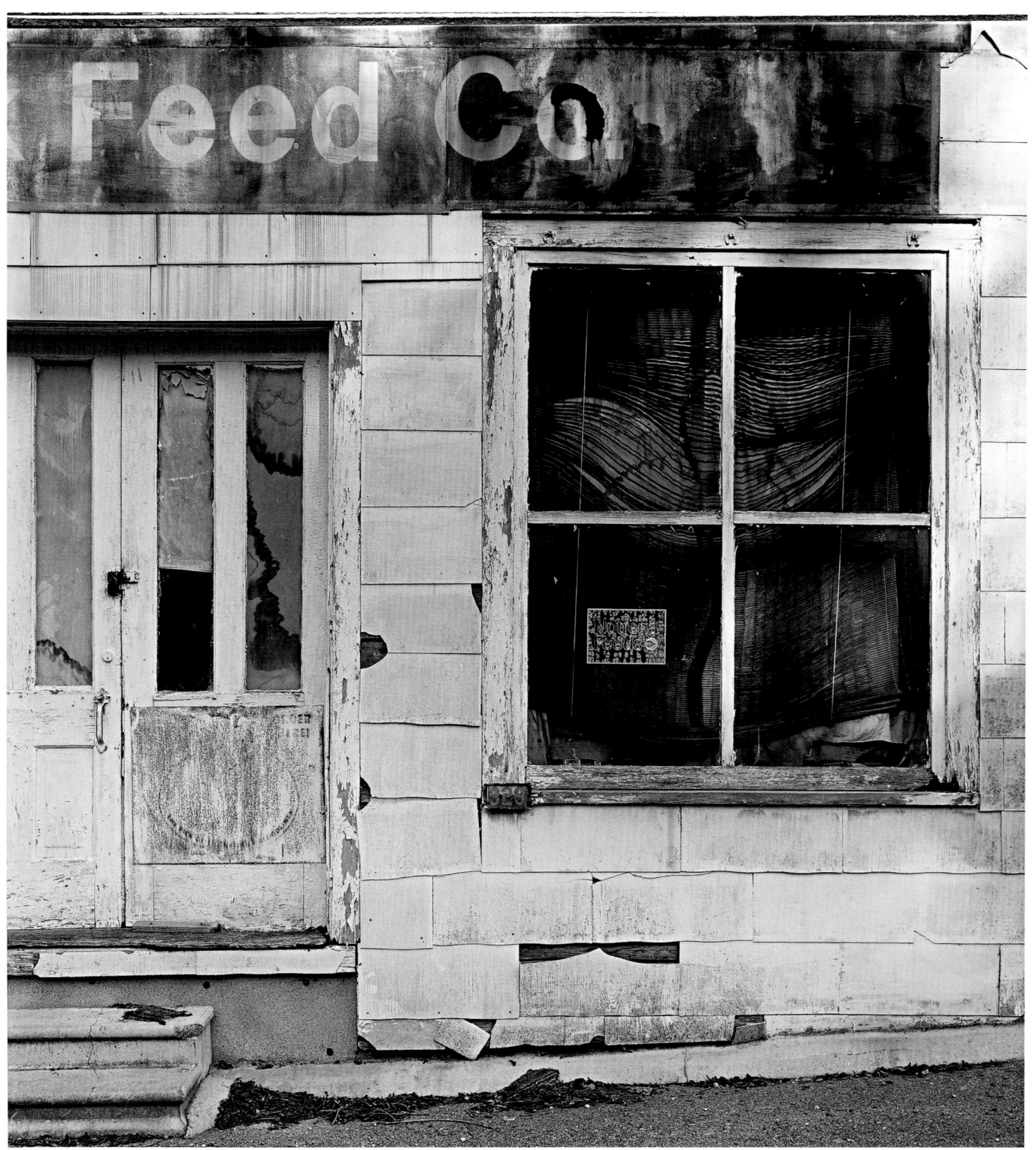

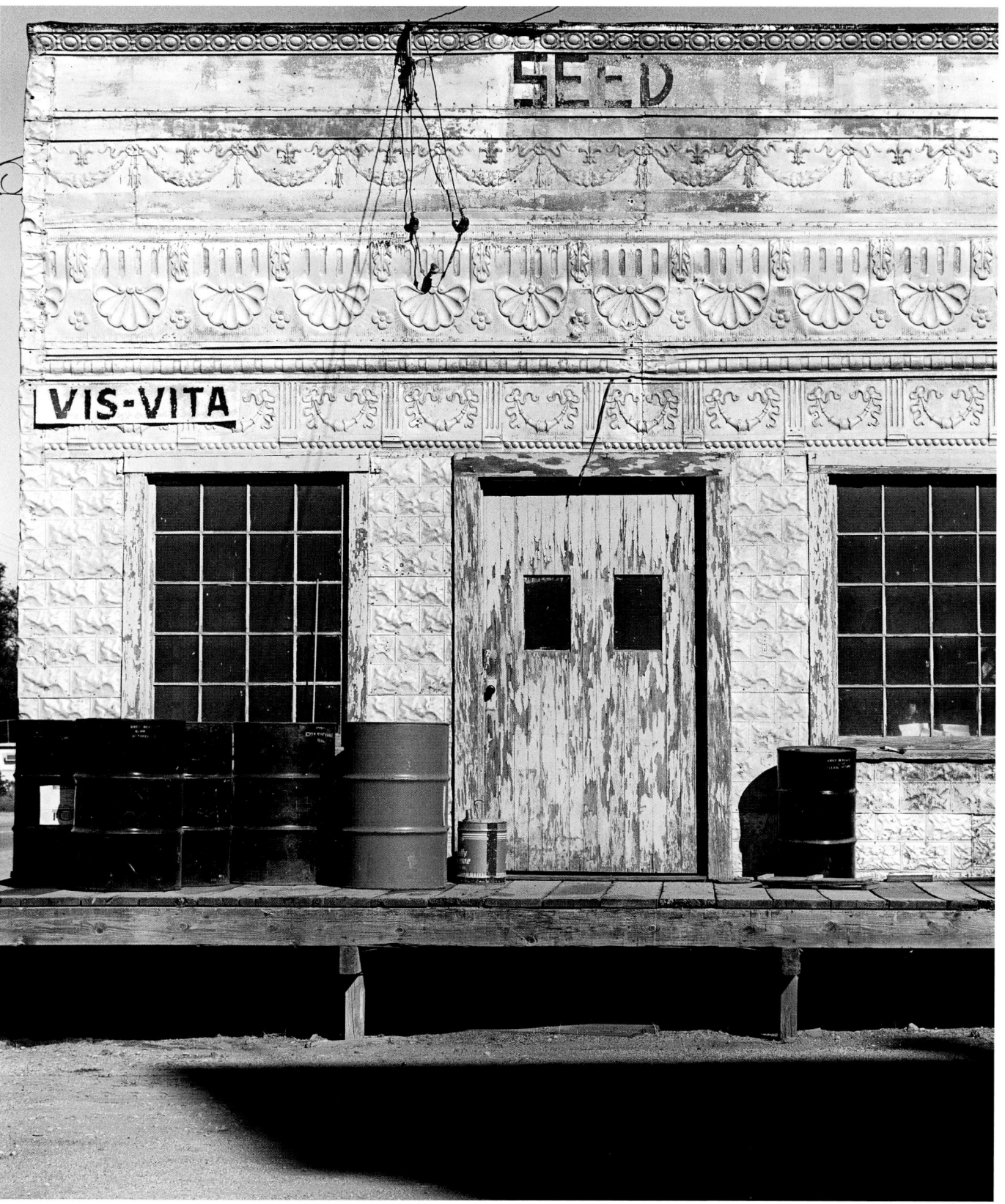

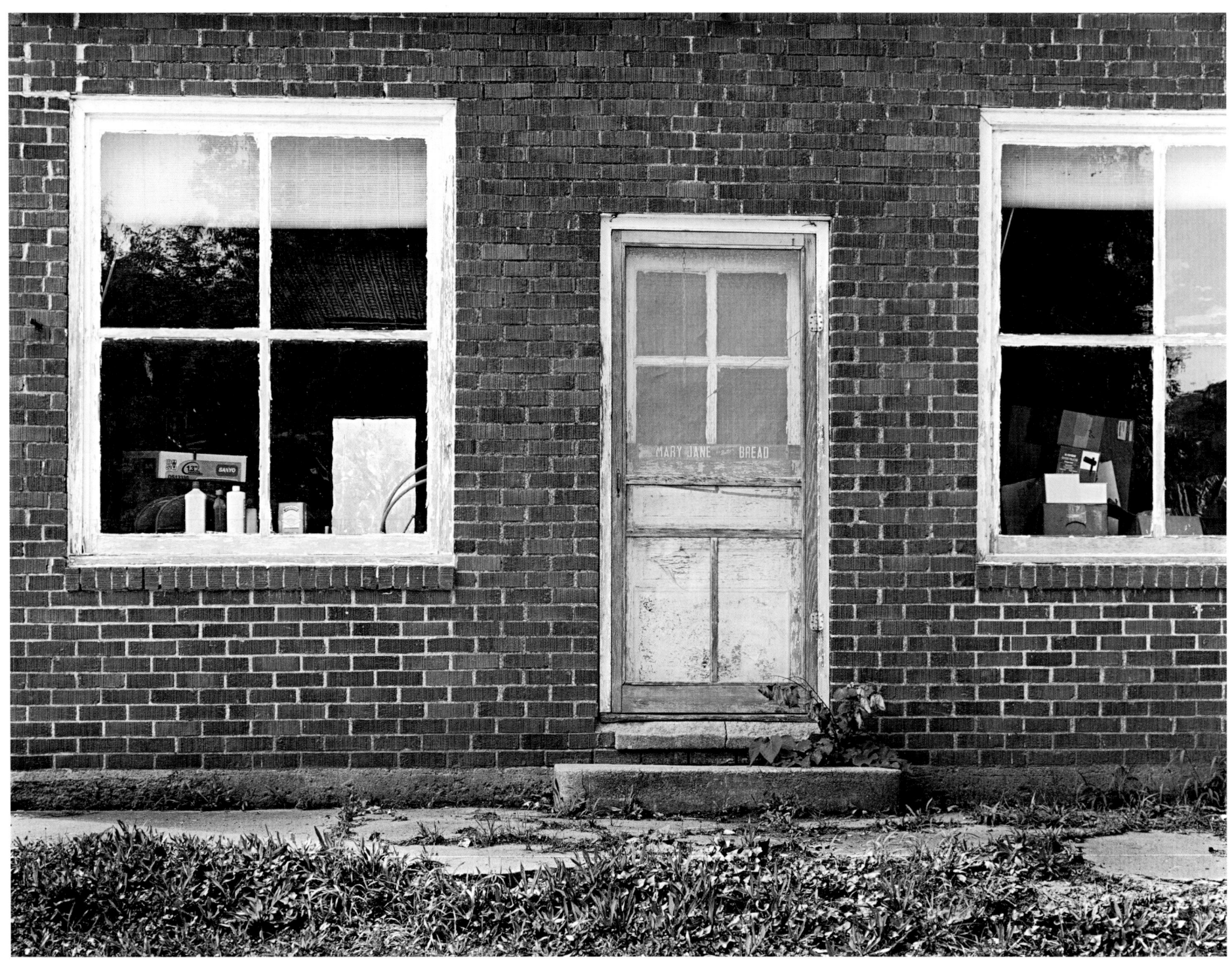

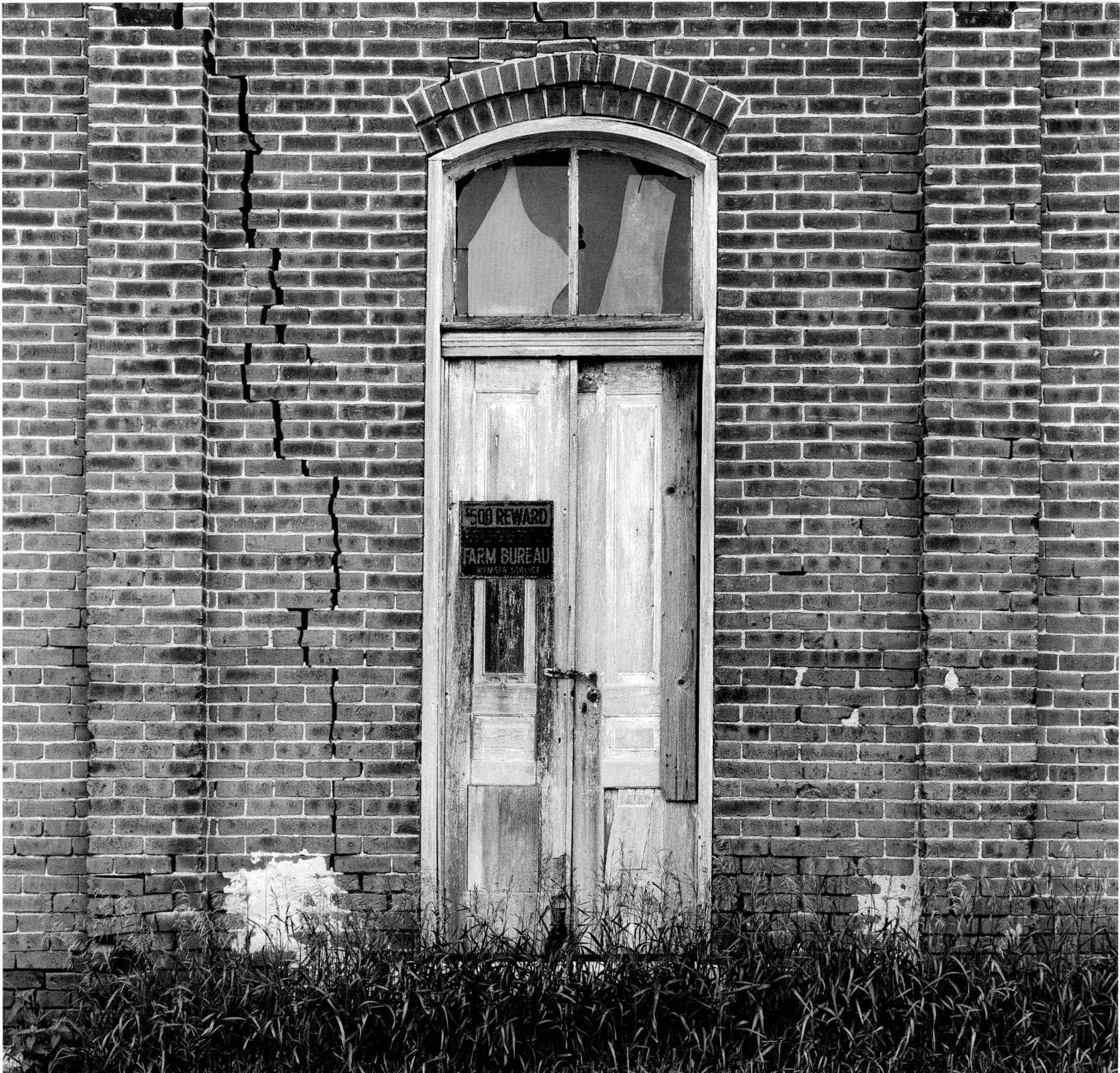

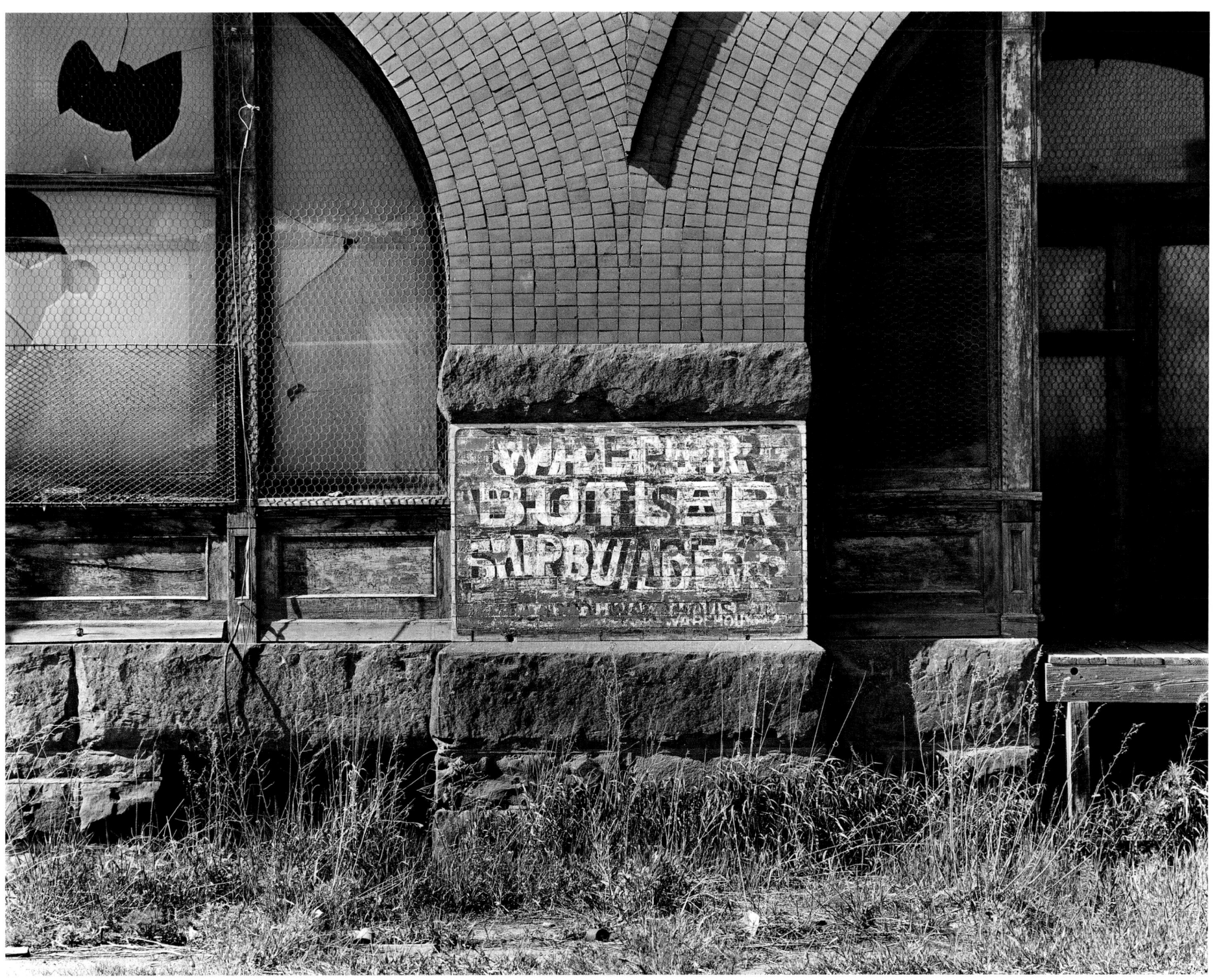

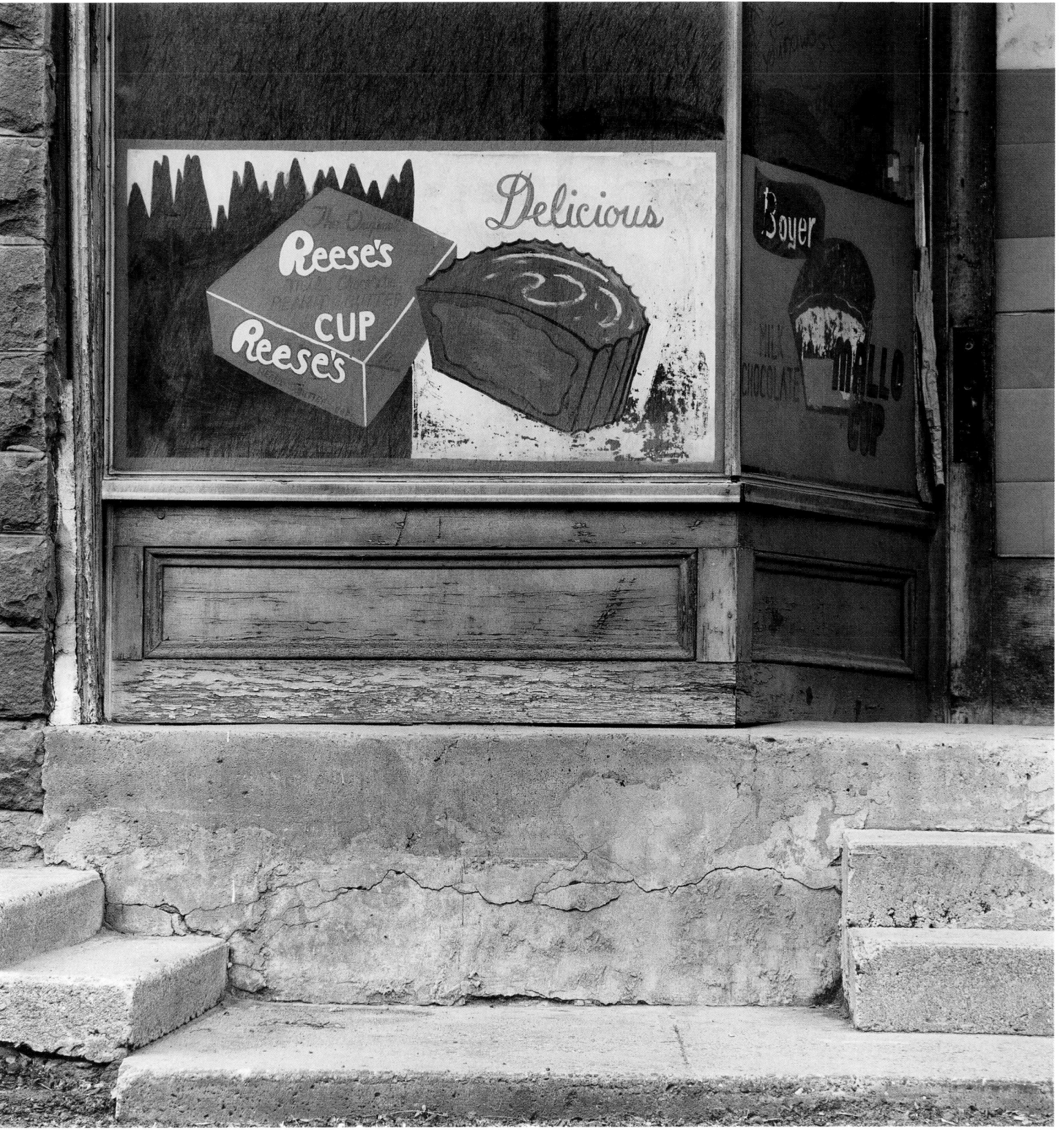

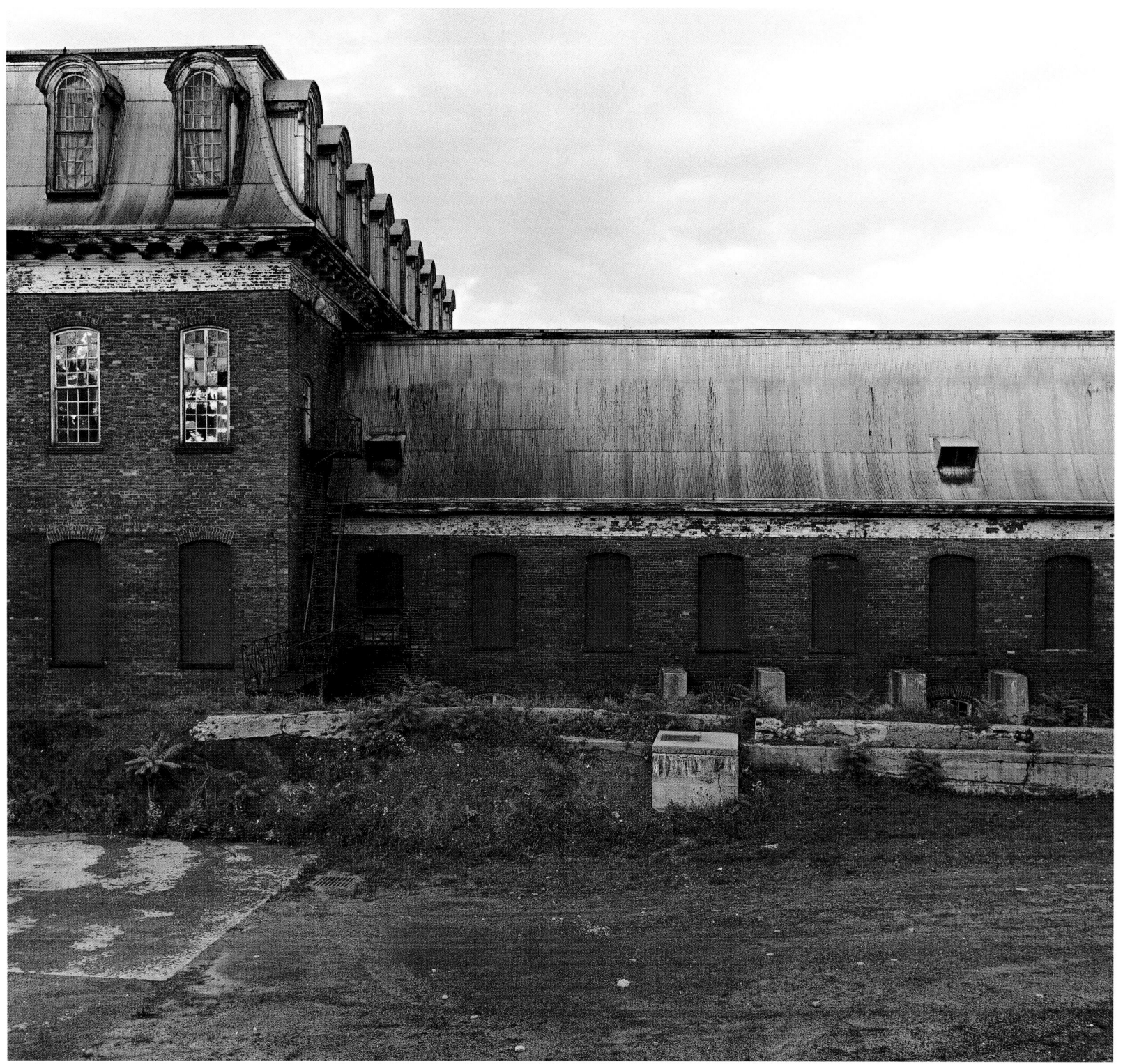

60 · Textile Mill, Cohoes, New York (1976)

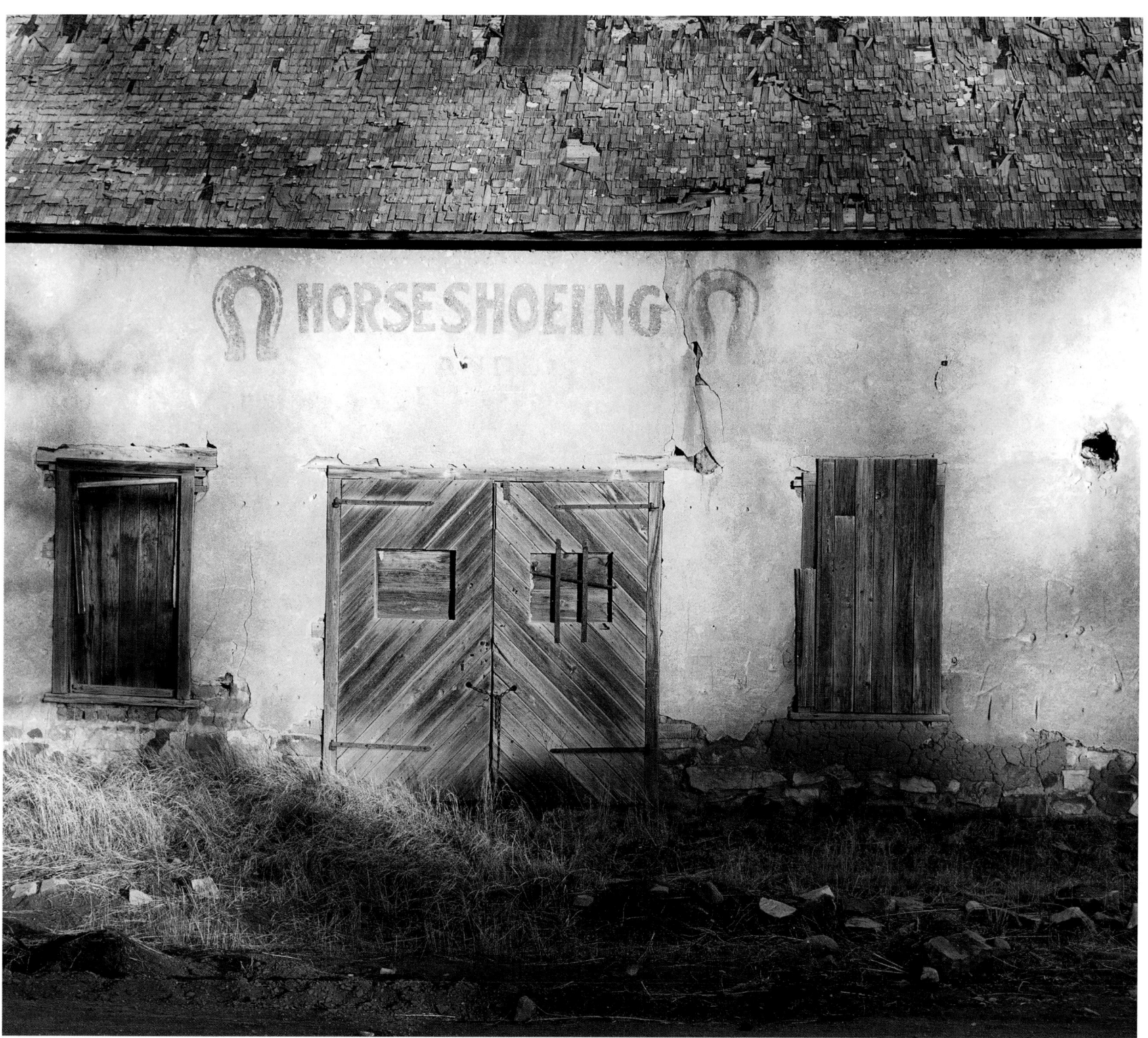

61 · Watrous, New Mexico (1972)

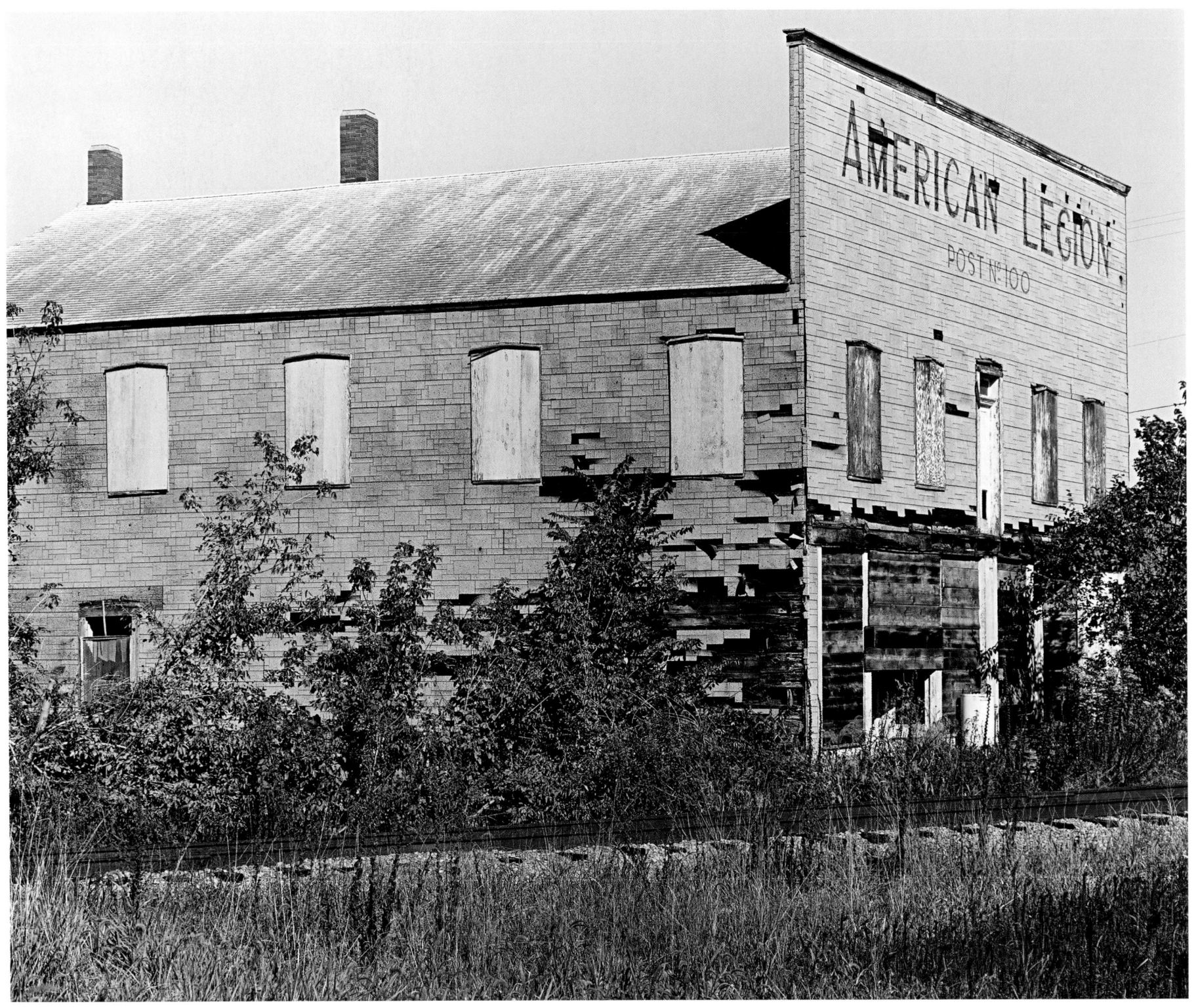

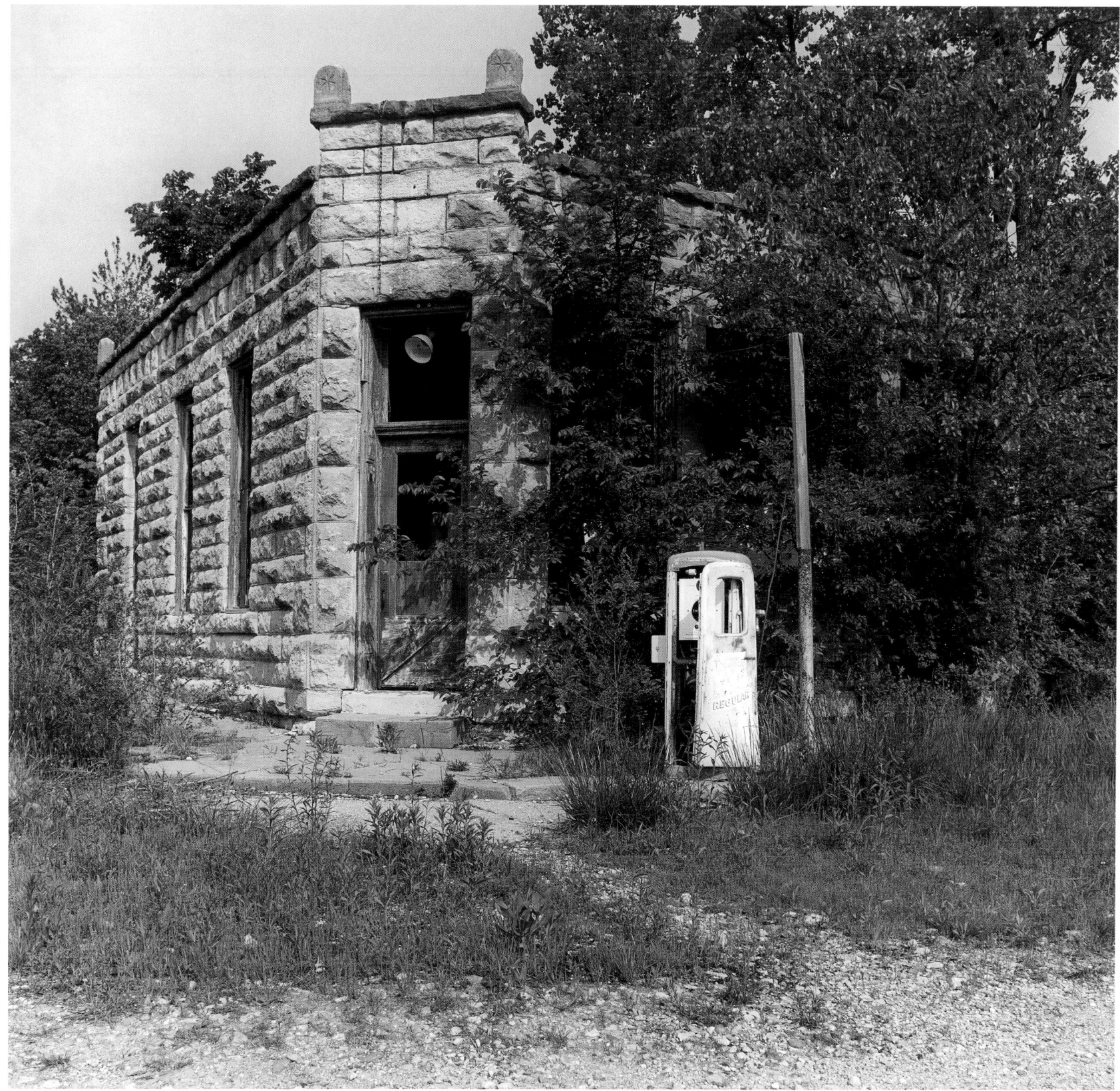

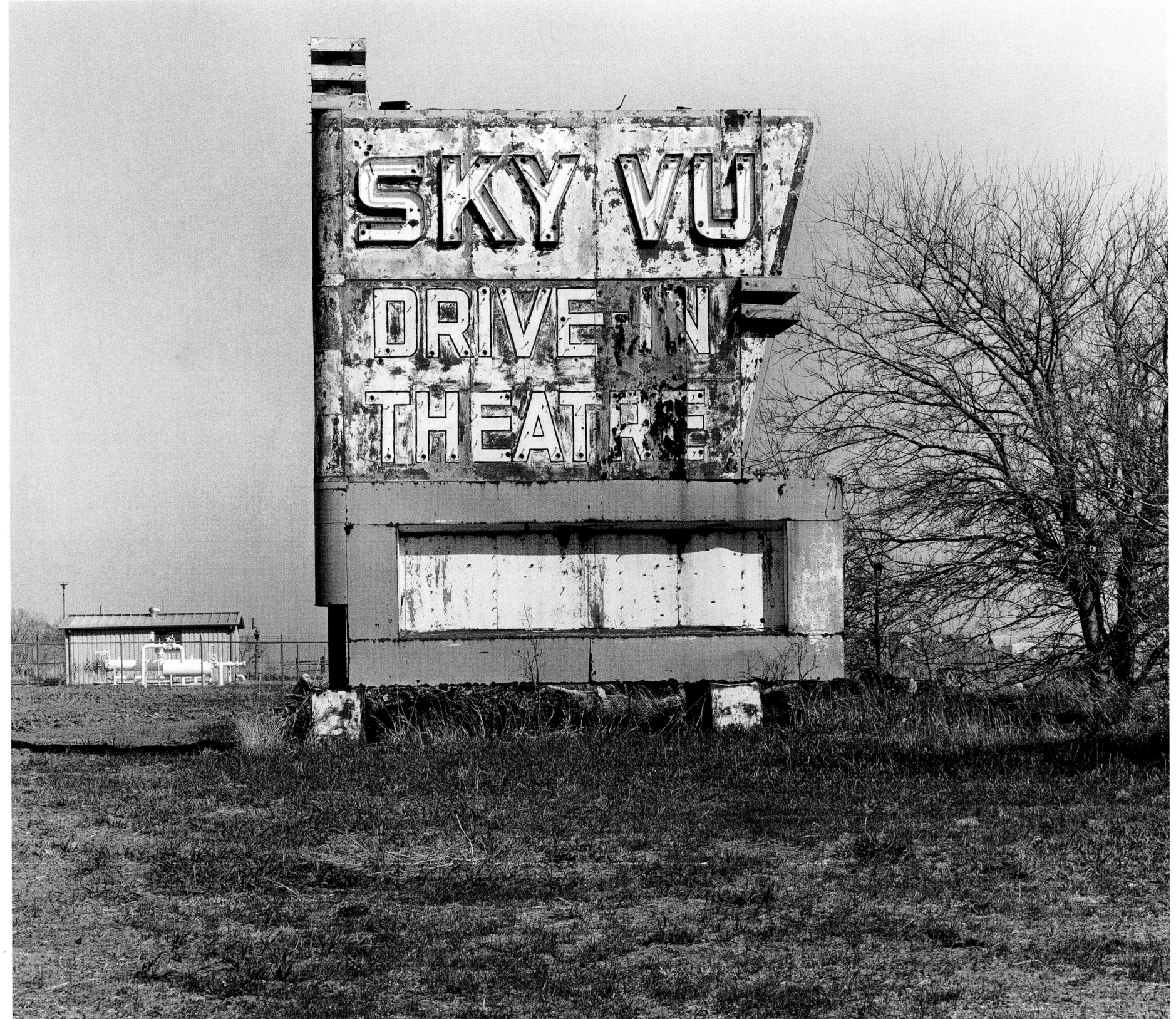

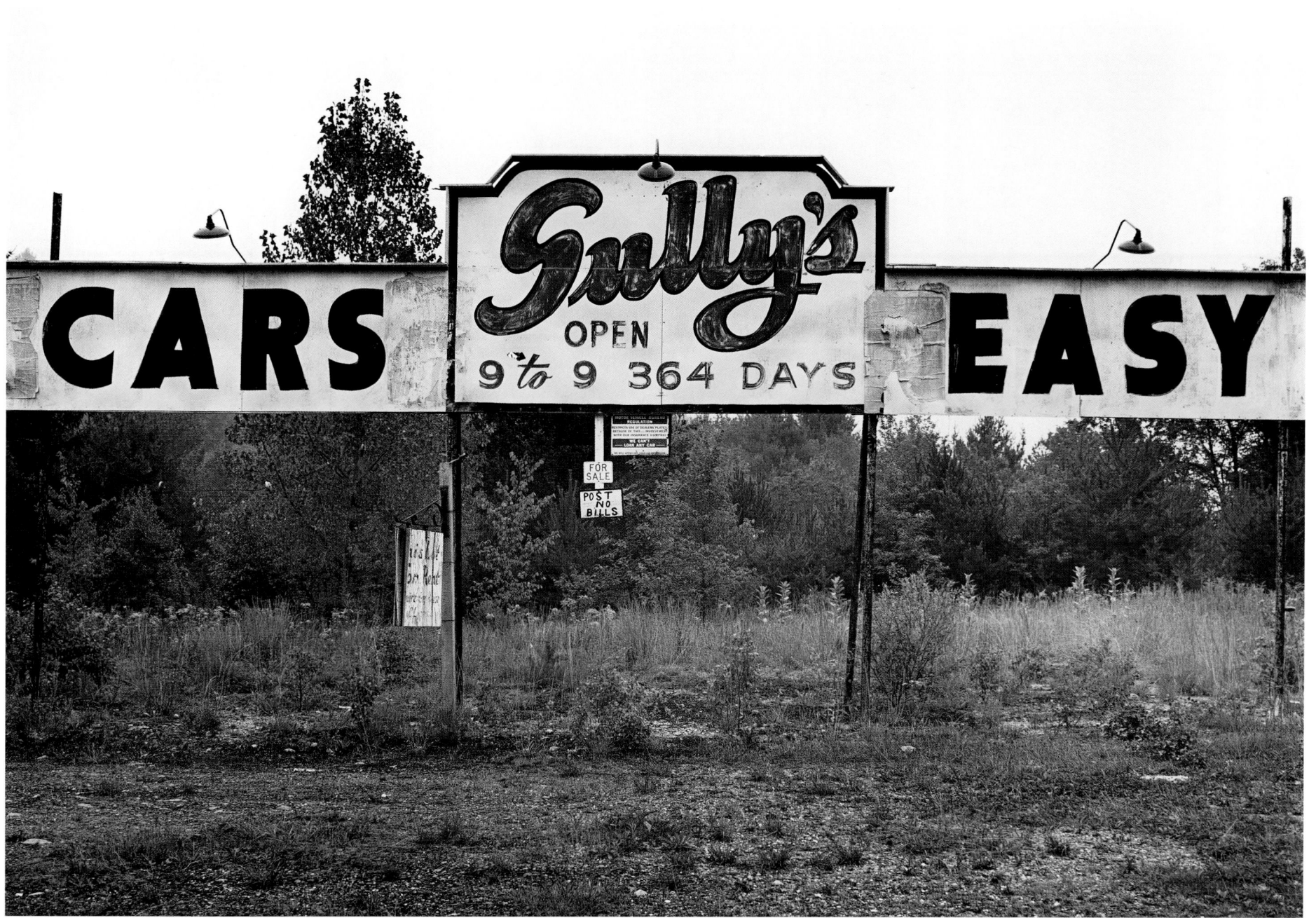

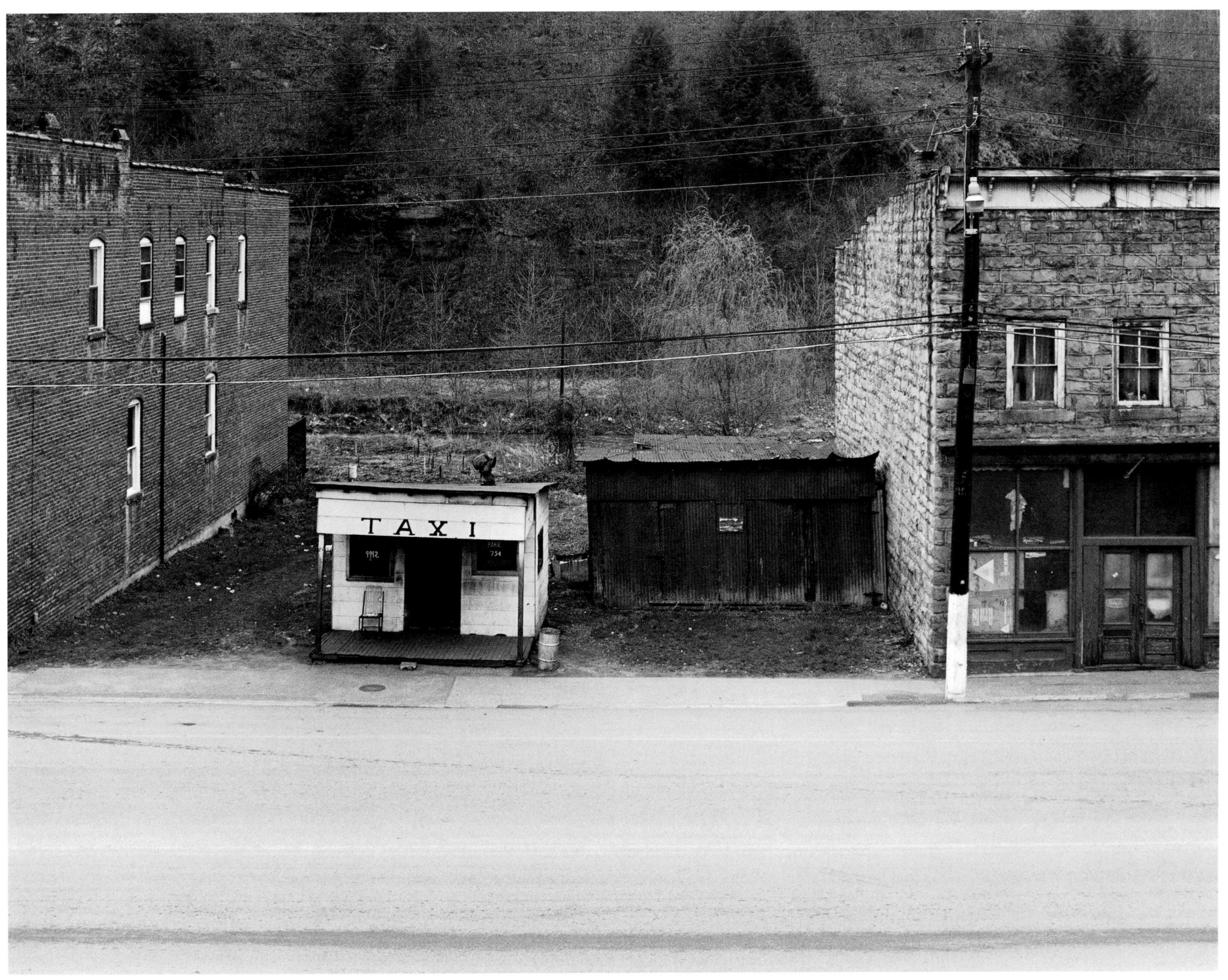

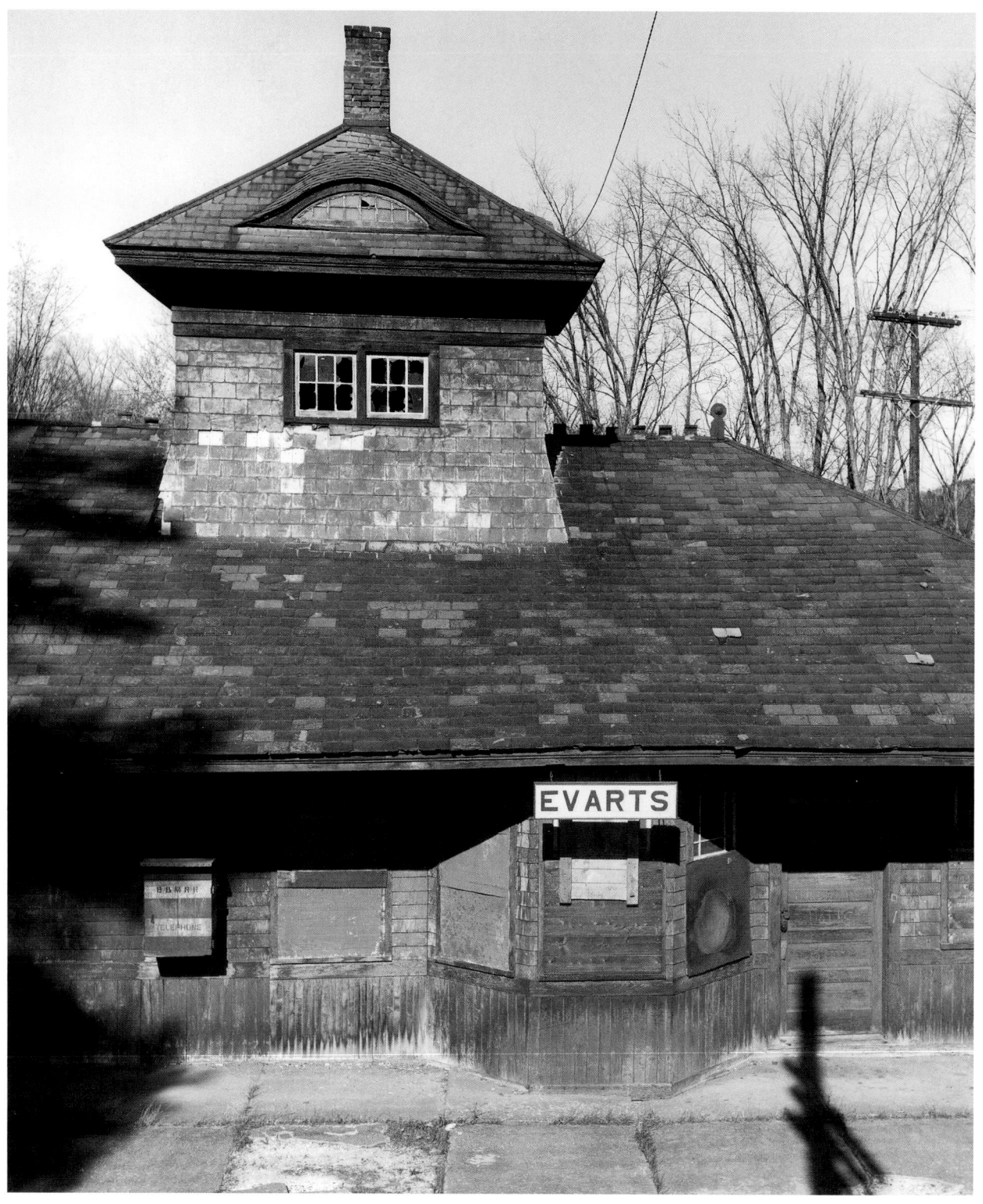

67 · Abandoned Depot, Evarts, Vermont (1962)   /   68 · Abandoned Depot, North Easton, Massachusetts (1965)

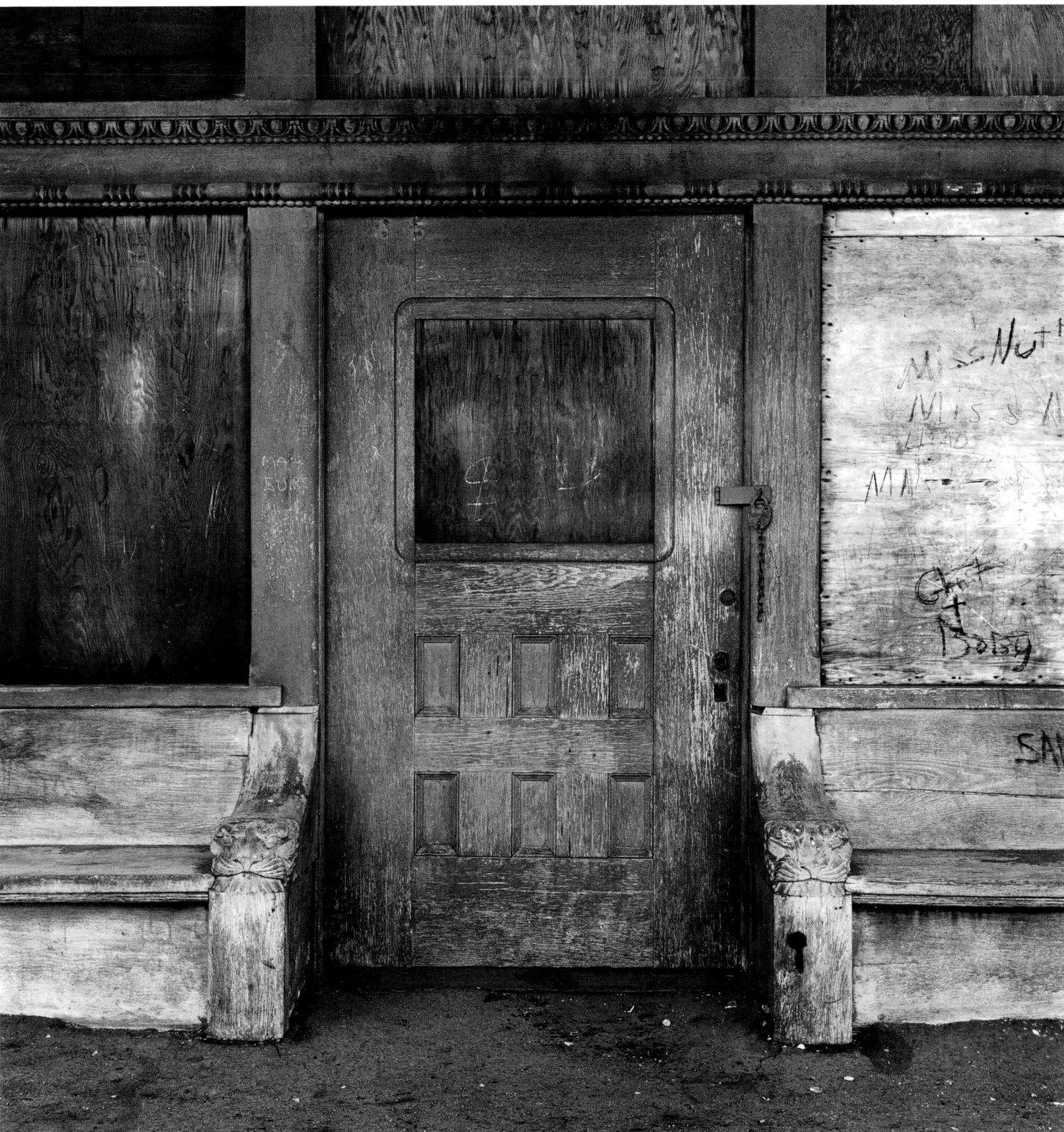

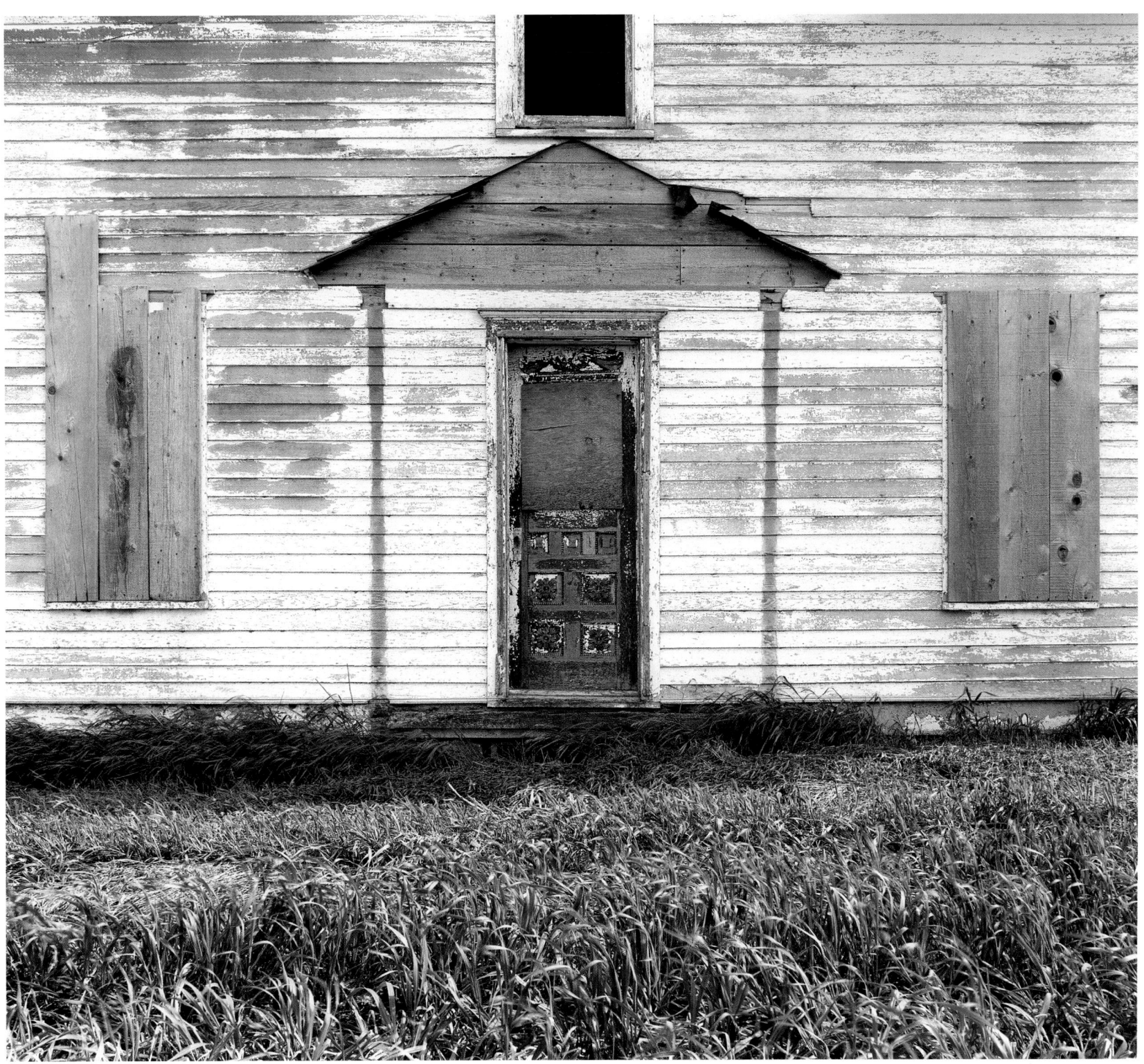

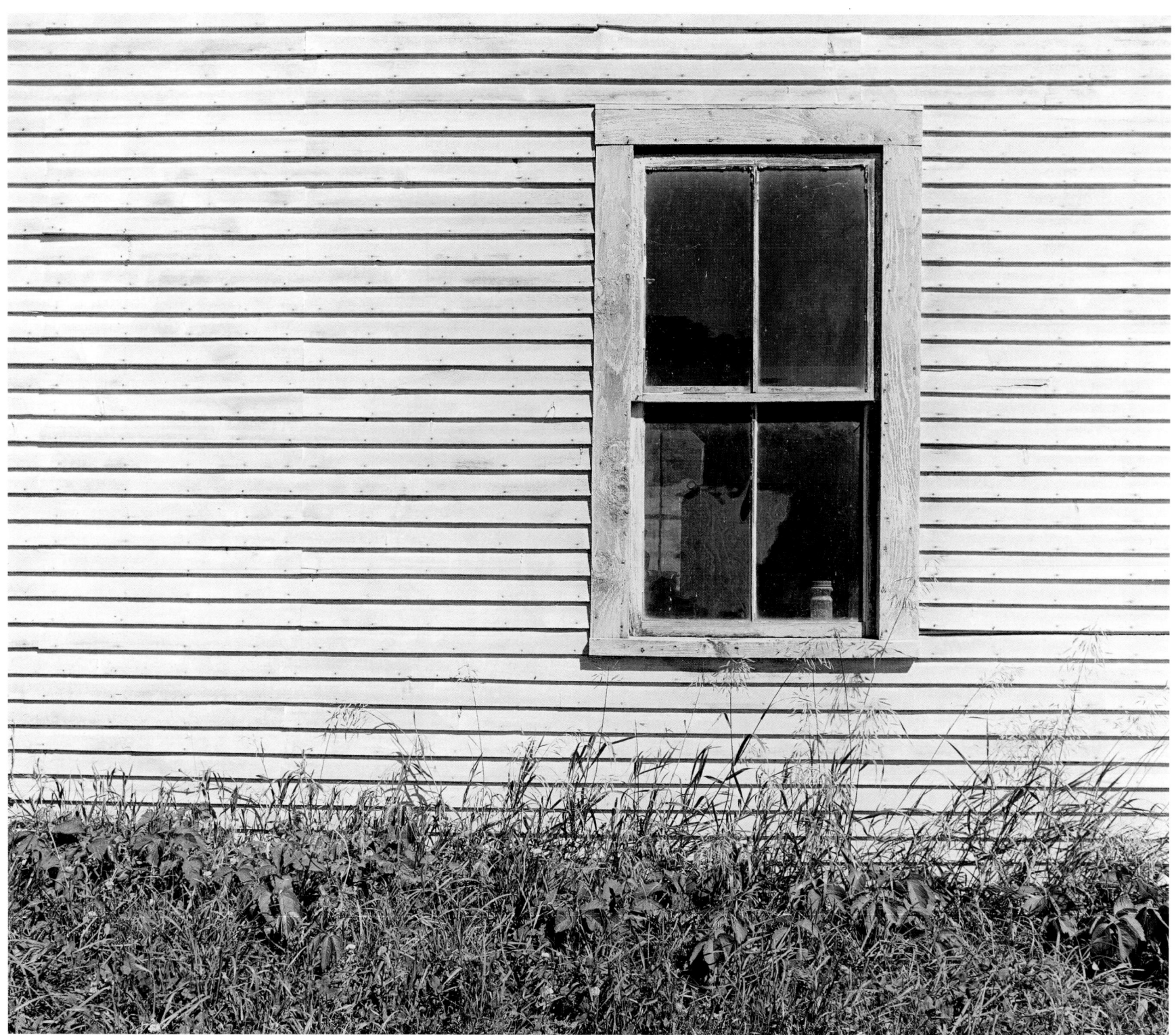

70 · Abandoned Barn, Tunbridge, Vermont (2001)   /   71 · Church Façade, Stillwell, Indiana (2003)

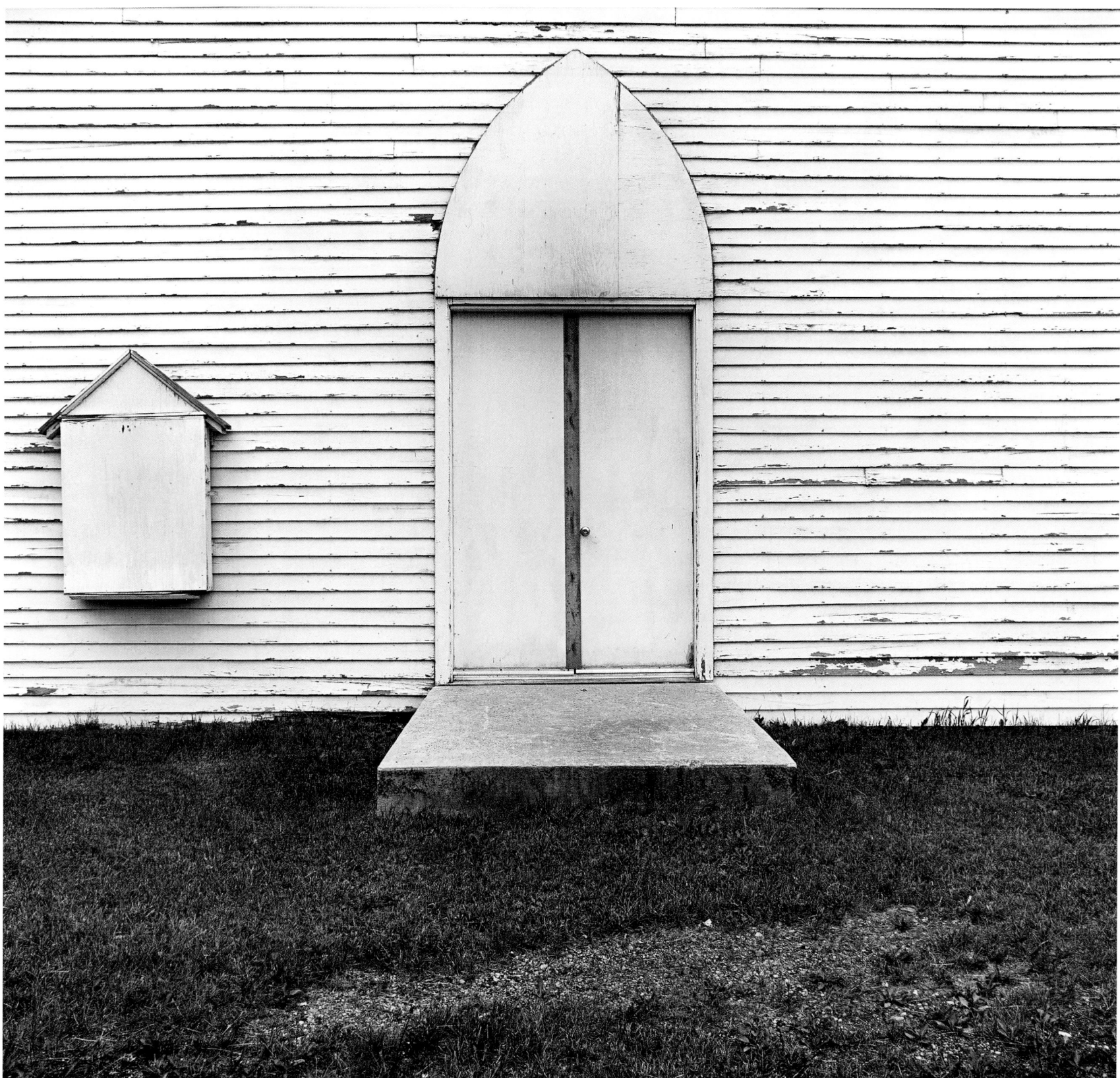

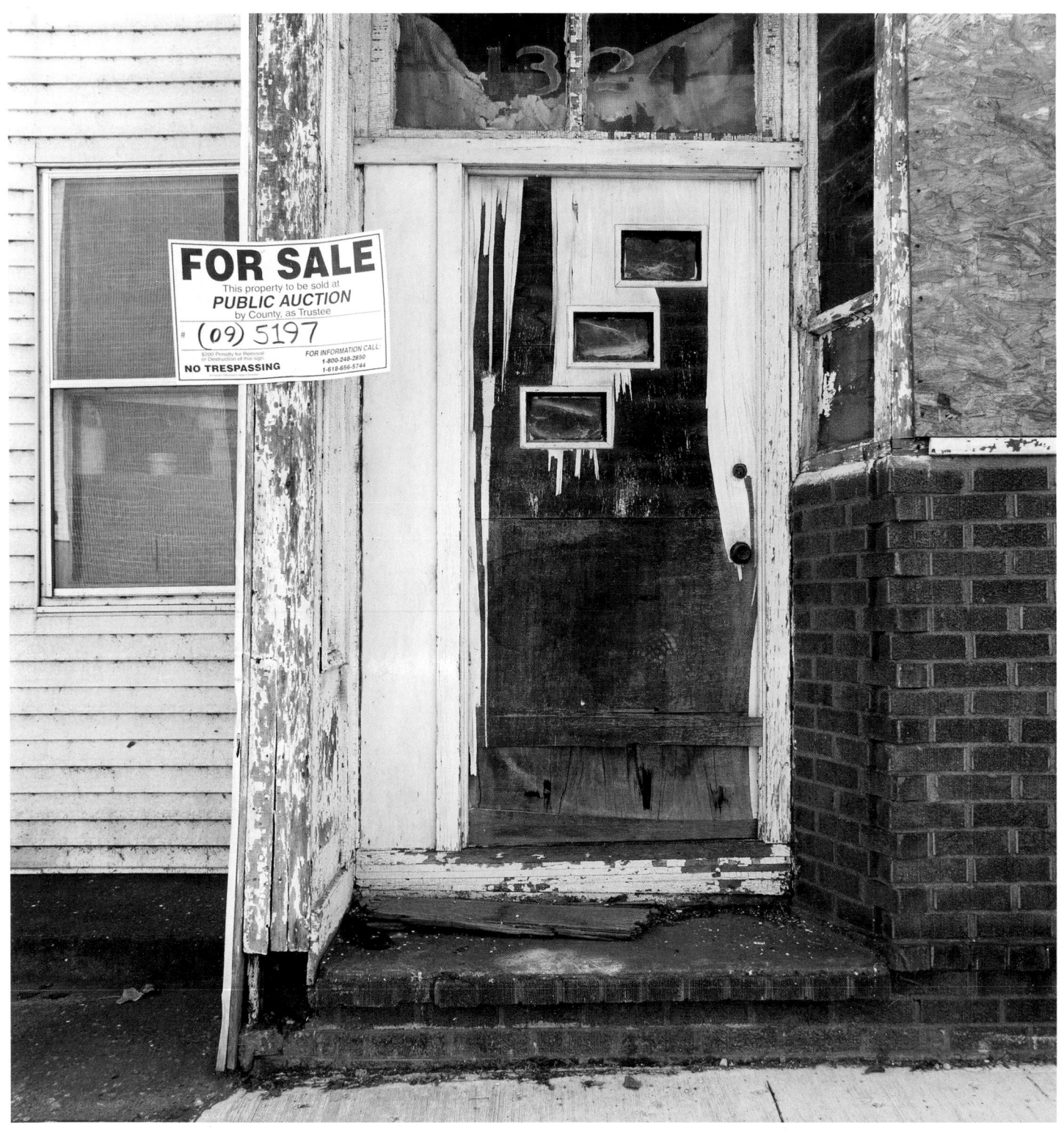

72 · Rock Island, Illinois (2003)   /   73 · Interior, Deserted Farmhouse, Montgomery County, Iowa (1987)

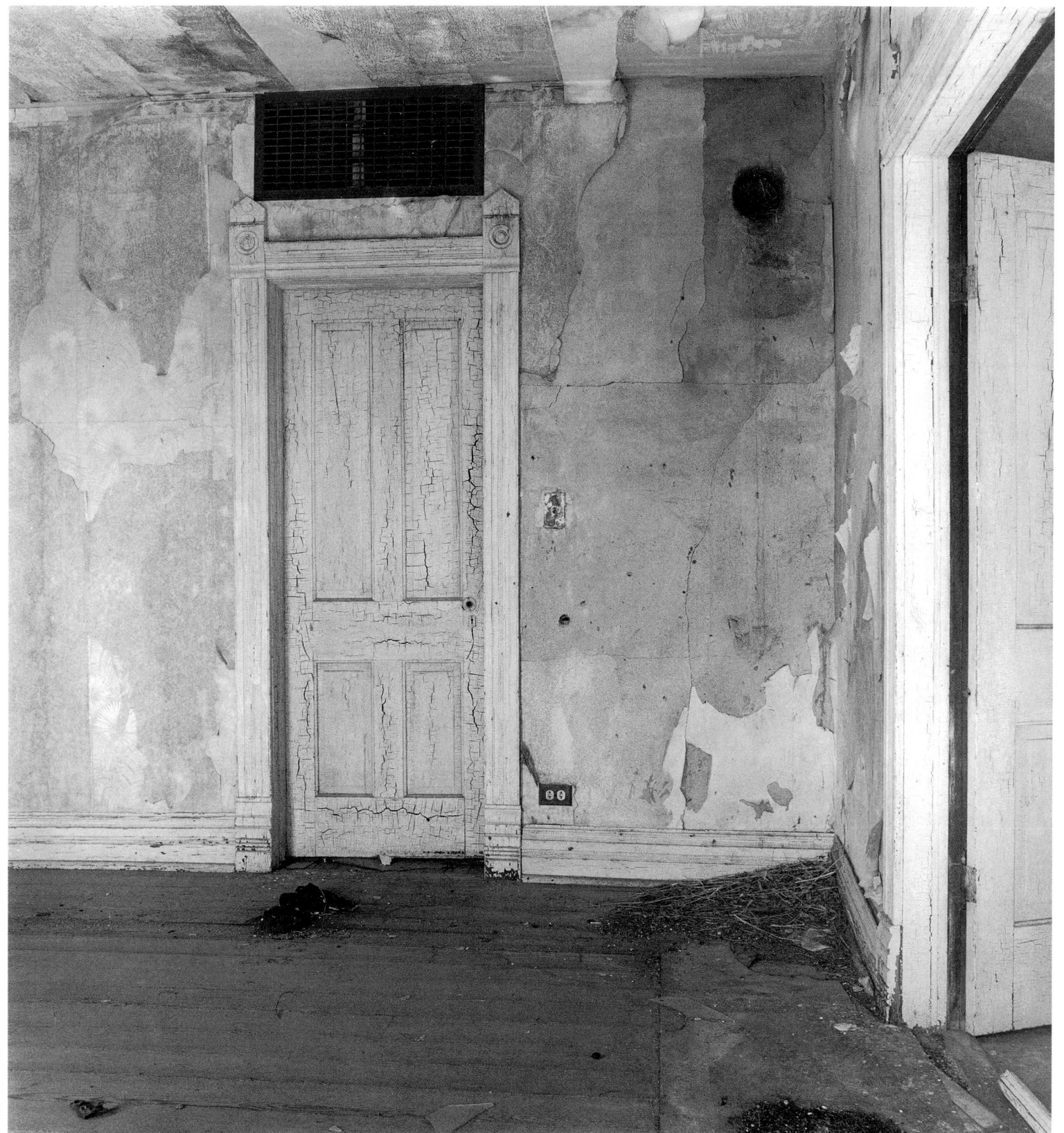

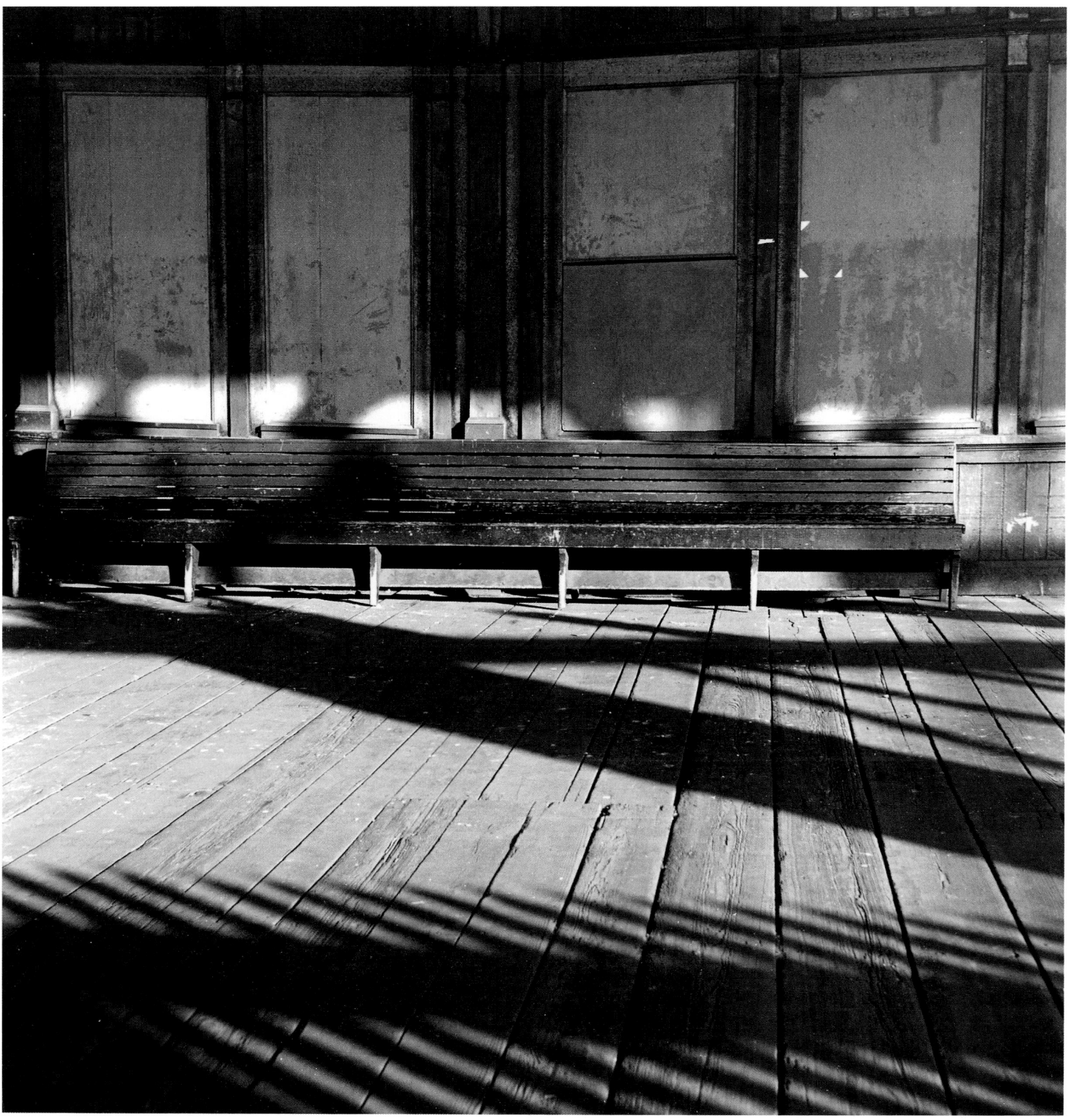

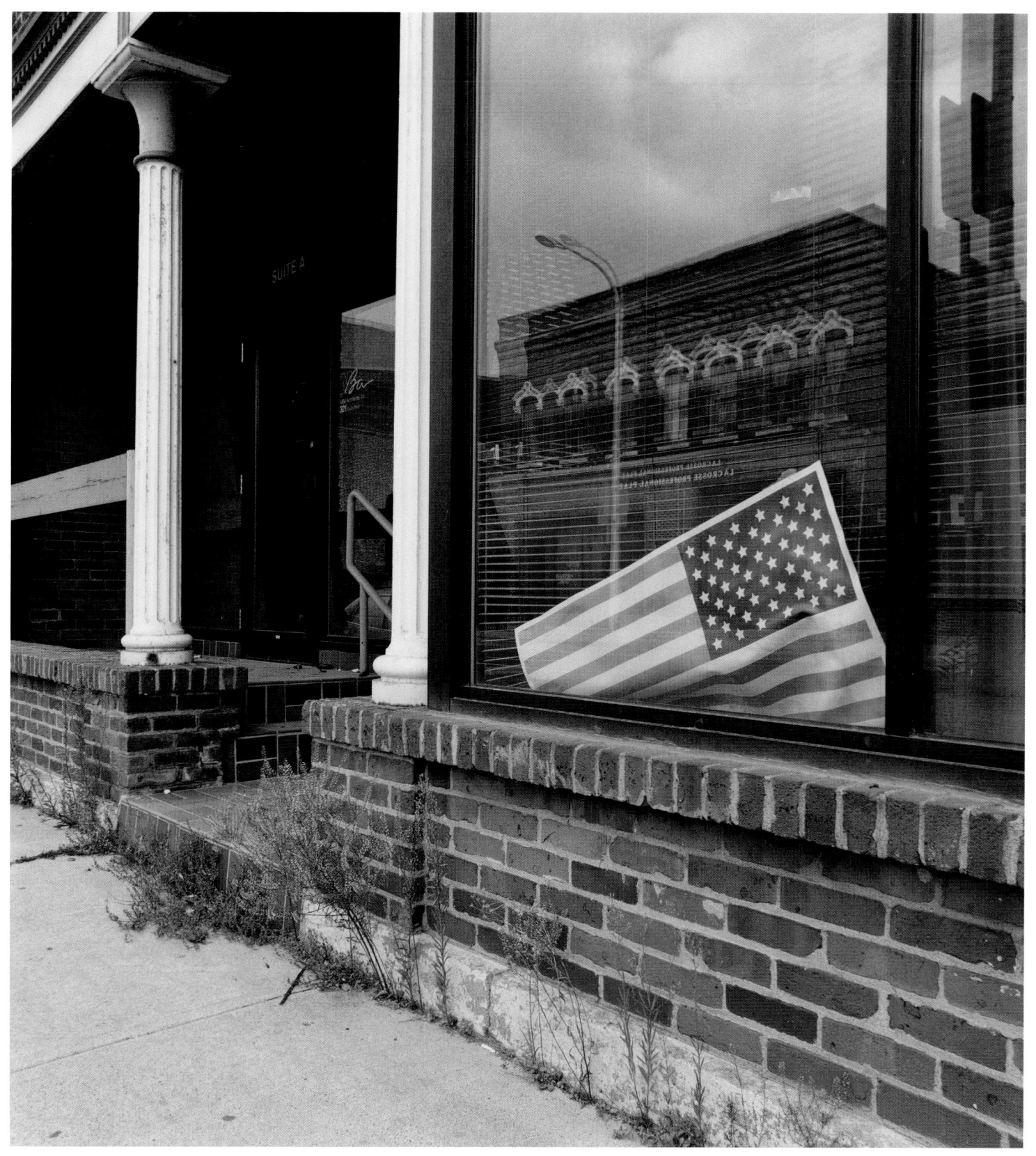

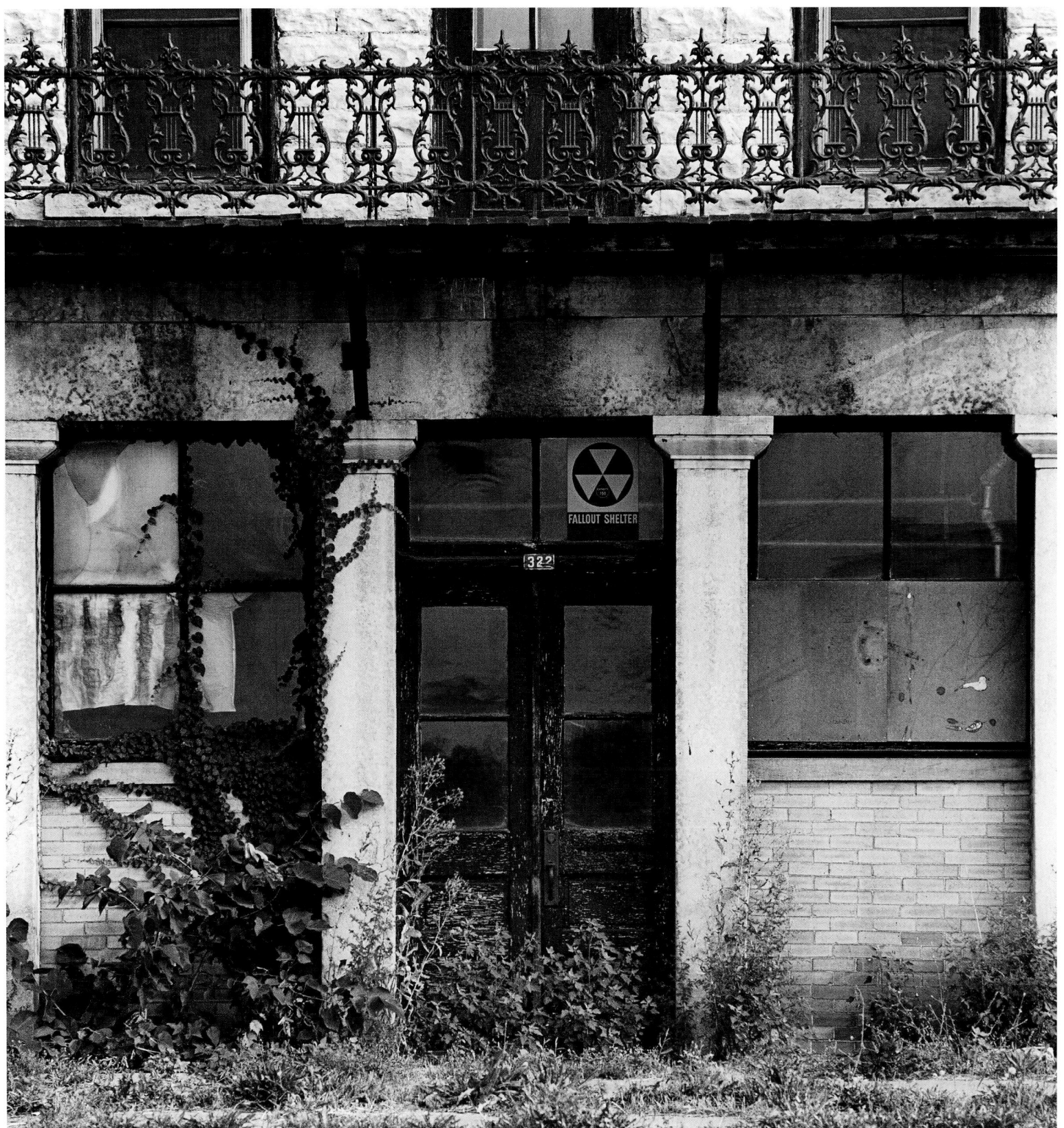

ACKNOWLEDGMENTS

I N 1964 I HAD A CALL FROM DAVID McCULLOUGH, who was then an editor at *American Heritage*. He told me he was looking for a photographer for an assignment and asked me if I would bring him some photographs. We made an appointment and I spent several days in the darkroom printing what I considered an appropriate selection. When I arrived at his office a few days later, the anteroom was filled with photographers, all of whom were older and obviously far more experienced than I. I waited until my turn came. David was very cordial. He looked at my pictures perfunctorily at first, with the eye of one who has already seen too many pictures. Then I noticed he was looking at them for a second time more and more slowly. He began to ask me a lot of questions. After the twenty minutes that is usually allotted to these appointments had elapsed, he stood up and started to escort me to the door saying, "I'll be in touch" and thanking me for coming in. I knew the drill well enough not to go home and sit expectantly waiting by the telephone. He opened the door. My heart sank. I saw the room full of waiting photographers. He hesitated a moment. His hand was still on the door. Then he shut it abruptly, turned to me, and said, "It's yours."

That assignment, to photograph the route of Abraham Lincoln's funeral train from Washington to Springfield, Illinois, a hundred years afterward was my first major commission. It was also a landmark. I discovered the rural Middle West, which I have photographed so extensively and come to love so deeply. It was then, too, that I realized how little remained from nineteenth-century American small towns and main streets—and how different America would be a hundred years hence. So, my old friend, McCullough, thank you for taking a chance on an unknown photographer and launching him on what has been a lifetime adventure of chronicling the ever-changing face of America. It is appropriate that one of the pictures I took on that assignment, the detail of the door of the church at Auriesville, New York, is reproduced in this book.

The pictures in this book are largely the result of serendipity. Collectively they are drawn from nearly forty-five years of exploring America. However, only two images have been previously published. Most have been made during the past fourteen years, and by far the majority of those during the numerous trips my wife, Sandra, and I made together in 2003 and 2004.

During my many years of exploration, there have been many individuals who have generously given their time, who took me into their confidence and went the extra mile to help with favors large and small. Although I can't remember all of you by name, to each and every one of you I give my heartfelt thanks.

There are a several people who have recently been most helpful to me with this project. First, I would like to thank Karen who answered the telephone at the post office in Gypsum, Kansas. When I explained who I was and what I was doing, she went to great lengths to help me. Because of her I was able to get in touch with Dale Claussen. When I asked about Carlton she looked up Patty Schlesener's number and suggested I call her.

I looked up Maurice Stroda on the Internet, whom I had known in Ramona fourteen years ago, and telephoned him. He had a hard time remembering who I was, nonetheless he and his wife—who I heard correcting him in the background throughout our conversation—answered many of the questions I had. It was nice to hear his voice again but sad to learn of that most of the people I had photographed in Ramona had died.

Without the invaluable assistance of Joe Byrnes during the last two years, it would have been impossible for me to have accomplished the enormous amount of work I have been able to do. Since September 2003 he and I developed 1,070 rolls of film. Then we numbered each frame, made contact prints of each roll before starting to make final the enlargements. All in all we printed more than 110 negatives. As I usually print only 2 negatives a day and make about a maximum of 30 prints, we made a total of approximately 3,300 11-x-14 prints. I did all the printing, developing, and toning. Joe ran the darkroom. He mixed all the chemicals, set up everything, managed to keep the temperatures on the money all day—no easy task. When the prints were dry, he pressed and spotted them.

I also want to thank my friend John Flak, who helped me on so many occasions in the darkroom and in the office before he moved away to Philadelphia. I miss you. Your wonderful sense of humor made many a long day possible.

A great debt of gratitude also goes to Liz Cockrum, Photo Shop wizard and organizer par excellence, who keeps the office machinery running and scans my photographs ad infinitum. You work harder than almost anyone I know to keep ahead of all I am forever asking you to do.

Once again I must thank Steve Serio, who always seems to come to my rescue at the eleventh hour when there is a job to get into FedEx by six o'clock or when there are two hundred prints to be spotted and Joe and I are working in the darkroom.

It very hard to find words to express my thanks to my editor, Jim Mairs. For nearly thirty years, you have been one of the most important people in my life and a true friend. You have always made me feel that you appreciate my work and have given me the confidence I have so often needed. Thank you for bearing with me. I know I am not the easiest person to work with, for I am never satisfied with my work, and you have always indulged my whims and been able to make a book in spite of me. A few months ago, Sandra and I sat around a huge table in Norton's New York office and watched you go to work on a pile of several hundred photographs that I had sent you. It was awesome experience. By the end of the day you had whittled the pile down to seventy-seven photographs—and the book was underway.

I would also like to express my thanks to Brook Wilensky-Lanford for always being so willing to help me and find the solutions to my multifarious questions and problems whenever I called you. Thank God she has a sense of humor.

I also feel I have driven the designer, John Bernstein, to distraction. This is our third book and I would imagine you would be quite happy if you never had to cope with my idiosyncrasies again. Be assured that I appreciate your efforts. Thank you!

Above all others, it is my dear wife, Sandra, who once again deserves the most credit of all. You and I conceived the idea together, and have worked together from the very beginning. I am the photographer, you kept reminding me. True. I fired the shutter. But we have been a team for twenty-eight years. Although you will categorically deny it, this book is in every way as much yours as mine. In 2003 and 2004 Sandra and I made numerous trips back and forth across the land throughout the American heartland. It was the first time we had had the chance to work in the field together. We drove thousands of miles, most of them off the beaten path on dusty section roads. I doubt if there was a town along the way we didn't explore. You eyes never stopped looking. "Turn around," you would frequently say. "I think there may be a photograph down that street." Nine times out of ten, you were right. Many of the photographs in this book were discovered by you. Not only did I rely on your eagle eyes but you were very fierce with me about keeping accurate records, something I tend to be a bit lackadaisical about. We never left a site without having made sure that every roll of film was numbered and all the technical data correctly entered in the logbook. You organized all the equipment—the lenses and films—so that whenever we saw a potential photograph everything was in place. We explored every day until dark and in the evening over dinner and a bottle of wine we would talk about what we had discovered and what we needed to find when we started out in the morning.

Even if you did not always agree with me you, you kept saying, "Make certain to express your feelings about what is happening to America." You always asked me the hard questions that made me think and rethink whether I was on track or not. You spent hours—days—helping me edit and re-edit the photographs and the text until it was finally right. In every way you were there for me, as you always have been, supporting me, rejoicing with me, sustaining me during those dark periods of self-doubt that so often plague me. Yes, this book is ours.

Those days we spent foraging for photographs were among the happiest experiences and greatest joys of my life. Frankly I never had more fun with anyone—nor was I ever so productive. I can't wait to set forth with you again!

You once gave me a little magnet that says, "Happiness is being married to your best friend." So true. How should I be so lucky?

TECHNICAL DATA

ALL THE PHOTOGRAPHS but two in this book were taken with 2¼" x 2¼" Hasselblad cameras, which I have used exclusively for my work since 1964. The two exceptions are the old New York Central Railroad ferry house in Weehawken, New Jersey, taken in 1961 and the abandoned depot at Evarts, Vermont, photographed in 1962. I used a Rolleiflex for both of these.

I have never been a "player" with different focal length lenses. I am usually able to decide on which lens is appropriate at the time I look at the subject. In fact, I know that it's time to "pack it in" when I start changing lenses every other minute.

Over the years I have discovered that I tend to use a wide-angle lens for most of my work—especially recently. No doubt this has to do with the square format, in which the foreground is a crucial part of the composition. For many years my "right eye" was a 60mm Zeiss lens. Now that Zeiss's 50mm lens is equally sharp I have relied on it for much of my work. However, where the situation is appropriate I use an 80mm, a 100mm, a 150mm, or, on rare occasions, a 250mm lens. I always use a cable release and a tripod. As far as I'm concerned, the tripod might as well be welded to my camera bodies.

Ever since I was fifteen, I have used the zone system of exposure. For many years I used various models of Weston meters; however, several of my photographic friends told me I was a dinosaur, to get with it and use a spot meter. They were right. I succumbed to their advice and for the last twenty-five years I have determined all my exposures with Zone VI analog spot meters. Incidentally, these are no longer made and my friends

probably still think I am back in the Cretaceous.

I learned darkroom technique from David Sapir and Timothy Asch at the Putney School in Vermont when I was fifteen. Since then I have always done all my own printing—except when a client calls for a print larger than 16 x 20 inches. I once had to have an immense print made of one of my photographs and took the negative to a custom printer. "I can make a better print than you can," said the man. "No doubt you may be a better printer than I," I replied. "But your print won't be mine. You weren't there when I took the picture. You didn't see what I saw." I should have reminded him of Ansel Adams's adage: "The negative is the score. The print is the performance."

Ever since the 1980s I have used a Zone VI cold light head to make all my enlargements. The model that I have used has, of course, been discontinued, so I have collected several cold lights and assorted parts from colleagues of mine who have gone digital. I have enough "spares" to keep me going until the day I am unable to stagger down to the darkroom.

I use Oriental Seagull graded paper exclusively—Grade 3— for 99.9999 % of my prints. Most of my prints are developed in Kodak Dektol developer at a temperature of 68 degrees plus or minus ³⁄₁₀ of a degree for a mean time of two minutes. I control the contrast by diluting the proportion of developer and water or by adjusting the time or a combination of both. I use a stop bath and two fixing baths and a Hypo clearing agent. All prints—even those that I eventually tear up—are toned in 2 to 4 ounces of Rapid Selenium Toner per gallon of water at 75 degrees. The prints are then washed for two hours in a Zone VI washer before being squeegeed and placed on screens to dry overnight.

I relied on Kodak Panatomic X film for 90 percent of my exterior work until it was discontinued in 1989. Once it was gone, I turned to Kodak T-MAX 100 and 400, which Kodak assured me was even better than Panatomic X. Not for me. After a year of increasing frustration, during which time I experimented with practically every known developer, I gave up on T-MAX. I tested several other films and on the advice of a colleague decided to use Kodak Verichrome Pan as the lesser of all evils. It was not the answer. I obtained increasingly mediocre results as the quality of that film began to deteriorate. One day a student of mine showed me her work. It was beautiful. "What kind of film are you using?" I asked? "Ilford," she replied. The lights suddenly went on. Wake up, Plowden! Where have you been? I immediately began making extensive tests with several Ilford films and discovered that their Pan-F was in many ways as good as Panatomic X. I rarely use a medium speed film, but when I do I will continue to use Ilford FP-4 as long as it is available. I used to rely on Kodak Tri-X Professional film (TXP 320) for all my interior work. However, it has recently been reformulated, and today I am learning to use Ilford HP-5 in its place.

I currently develop all my film in Kodak D-76, diluted 1 part water to 1 part developer at 68 degrees plus or minus $^{3}/_{10}$ of a degree.

Recently there have been a number of problems with Ilford's quality control—an endemic problem with all manufacturers of photographic material. Last year the company declared bankruptcy and it seemed probable it would discontinue manufacturing all its traditional photographic material. (Since then its film and paper division has been sold and production has been resumed.) Pan-F is the last fine-grain film available for the Hasselblad and I decided to hedge my bets. I bought three thousand rolls and froze it. Incidentally, I have been freezing all my materials since the mid-1980s, including the Oriental Seagull photographic paper so hopefully I can continue to print as long as I am able to work.

I have often been asked whether I ever use artificial light. No. I never want to disturb the light. All my exposures are made with available light. I have never used a strobe or a flash—or for that matter a filter of any kind. I have also been asked whether I ever crop my images, as if it would be some sort of mortal sin to do so. Of course I do. All photographers do. Every time we make a photograph we crop out a piece of the world. In my case I form the final print—whether it be square, horizontal, vertical, or something in between—in the ground glass on location before I fire the shutter. I know precisely what the final image will look like before I go into the darkroom—and which ones I will ultimately print. The only surprises in the darkroom are disasters resulting from some dreadful technical miscalculation—which I assure you still happens after nearly sixty years of experience.

PLATES